THE MILLIONAIRE ZONE

THE
MILLIONAIRE ZONE

✦ *Seven*
Winning Steps
to a
Seven-Figure
Fortune

JENNIFER
OPENSHAW

NEW YORK

ISBN: 1-4013-0325-0
ISBN-13: 978-1-4013-0325-9

Hyperion books are available for special promotions and premiums.
For details contact Michael Rentas, Assistant Director, Inventory
Operations, Hyperion, 77 West 66th Street, 12th floor, New York,
New York 10023, or call 212-456-0133.

Design by Victoria Hartman

FIRST EDITION

1   3   5   7   9   10   8   6   4   2

To everyone
who has ever dreamed
of a better life

The Research for The Millionaire Zone

To better understand how millionaires achieve their financial success, as well as to understand what holds other Americans back from that kind of success, the author hired two independent research firms to conduct two surveys. In all, more than 3,000 Americans were surveyed.

The first survey was conducted by Harris Interactive among working Americans. This survey was conducted online between July 19 and July 21, 2006, among 2,653 U.S. adults 18 years of age or older. The results were weighted for region, age, gender, education, household income, and race/ethnicity to match them to their actual proportions in the population.

The other survey was conducted by Chicago-based Spectrem Group. This survey was of 500 high-net-worth Americans via telephone. The respondents all had investable assets of at least $500,000. The respondents were then separated to create results for two groups: those with a net worth of $1 million or more, excluding the value of their primary residence; and those with a net worth of less than $1 million. The results for the first group are generally reported in this book. However, where referenced, results have also been reported for the second group, to highlight additional insights.

Another survey of approximately 50 owners of companies with revenues averaging $11 million was conducted by the author.

In addition, the author accessed publicly available information on select members of the Forbes 400 Richest Americans list to identify those who have used and applied the strategies discussed in this book. She also relied on more than 100 interviews with wealthy Americans.

Acknowledgments

Just as you need your LifeNet to reach the Millionaire Zone, so too did I need my LifeNet to launch *The Millionaire Zone*! I'm enormously grateful to the Americans who've inspired me over the years—readers, viewers, seminar attendees. You and your stories touch me daily and keep me passionate about what I do. Please keep sharing!

At ABC Radio, I want to thank Kevin L. Miller for his belief in me, for truly being a partner, and for lighting a fire under me to do this book. Thanks also to John McConnell, George Spanos, Corney Kohl, and Keven Bellows—you have all been enormously supportive in my radio endeavors.

For seven years, I've written for MarketWatch.com, now a division of Dow Jones, and have had the great pleasure of working with such high-caliber people as editor-in-chief Dave Callaway and editor Steve Kerch. My friends at AOL's Money & Finance section—Bill Wilson, Marty Moe, Steve Gaitten, Jamie Hammond, Alan Halprin and Amey Stone, Jennie Baird, and Alysia Lew—you've all been terrifically creative, open-minded, and supportive. Thank you!

When I met the publishers and editors at Hyperion—Bob Miller, Ellen Archer, and my editor, Gretchen Young—I was overwhelmed by their enthusiasm. It's the kind I talk about in the book. That's how I knew I was home. Every day as a question came up or a need arose, you've been right there, always being your best so that I could be mine. It has made all the difference.

Special thanks to Marcia Firestone, founder of the Women Presidents' Organization, and Jim Weldon, a long-time friend and entrepreneur, who connected me to some of those featured in this book. Deanna Percasi and Kathy Steinberg at Harris Interactive and Cathy McBreen and Tom Wynn at the Spectrem Group brought invaluable expertise and professionalism to our surveys.

I work daily with several people who help make it all happen. Charlie Benard, whose knowledge, experience, and belief in me in the early days have been a source of strength. Thanks go to Peter Sander and his wife, Jennifer, who worked with me on my first public television show, for bringing your terrific editing skills to my work and for always so graciously sharing your creative minds. My brother Jeff Openshaw is my audiovisual guru, and Rosa Maulini has provided administrative support for some seven years now. Maureen Monfore, research assistant on this book, enriched it with marvelous features of many on the Forbes 400 Richest Americans list. Andrea Coombes, a dear friend who brought life to my words—I don't know how we did it so quickly, but we did, thanks to you!

My mother and father, Rosemary and Pete, continue to be a great support and inspiration. I thank you for being there every day with your words of love and encouragement. Mom Bette, Amy, and Reed—my East Coast family—have made my move from the West Coast simply a redefinition of my Comfort Zone—with all the accoutrements that go with it!

Finally, to my better half, Randy Schwimmer, who blesses me every day in ways I never imagined possible. You have been a partner in this entire project, and so much more. You brought your incredibly creative mind and superb editing skills to this endeavor. You were patient and understanding when there were deadlines to be met. And, always, you shared my passion for the ideas in this book. Not a day goes by when I don't see, through you, the power of using one's LifeNet.

Contents

Introduction

I'm on National TV

I've just finished taping a national television show before a live audience, and I'm pumped, really pumped. As I walk offstage, Cher's "Believe" blasts at high volume. The 300 people in the audience are keyed up by the lights, music, cameras. The families who shared their heart-wrenching stories about their financial lives moved us all. I feel like I've made a difference.

As I move past the control room where buttons are pressed and levers are pulled to make the magic of national television come into your home, a sea of people comes up to me, peppering me with questions.

"Should I invest in real estate?"

"How can I get rid of my credit card debt?"

"What do I do with my inheritance money?"

"Should my husband and I have separate checking accounts?"

People ask me these types of questions all the time.

But then a woman in her mid-forties, attractive with brown medium-length hair, comes up to me.

"Jennifer, my name is Laura and I loved the show," she gushes. "It was really helpful. Tons of information. I'm really motivated. But . . ."

I knew there was a "but" coming.

"So how can I help you?" I ask.

The look on her face suddenly changes. Now, instead of excitement, I can see fear in her eyes. It's a look I've seen before. Many times.

Laura hesitates a moment. "Well, I want to move forward. I want to make money, provide for my family, and create a real safety net."

"So what's holding you back?"

"I just don't know where to start," she says. "I feel frozen. I'm confused. I've read a lot of those books out there but I'm still left feeling like . . . well, like it's all on my shoulders. And frankly, it's pretty scary."

My Eureka! Moment

That's when it struck me. I had been accumulating evidence for many years, but for some reason Laura's sincerity and intensity brought it home to me: Real financial success—making money—is not a tax issue, an insurance issue, or a stocks vs. bonds issue. In fact, it's not about money at all. It's about fear. The road to the Millionaire Zone, as I call it, is all about overcoming the anxiety about changing your life, yet operating in a familiar place so you can shift your future from neutral into high gear.

But how do you do that? How do you un-stick yourself and join those millionaires in the Millionaire Zone so you can reach your dreams?

That's what this book is all about. Whether you're in a job wanting to move up or out, an entrepreneur looking to expand your opportunities, or someone with an idea or a passion looking to turn it into profits, I'm going to arm you with a set of strategies and practical advice that will help you reach these goals. I'm going to do it by changing your thinking and empowering you with tools already at your disposal. Believe me, my system *will* make a big difference in your life.

Over the last seven years, ever since I sold my first financial services company and reached the Millionaire Zone myself, I've been on a personal mission—a mission to understand what distinguishes those who make it from those who don't.

I've spent years meeting and interviewing the rich to understand how they did it when many of them started with nothing—no money, no inheritance, no sugar daddy.

I've sailed on yachts with some of the Forbes 400 Richest Americans, I've been in Silicon Valley building my own company, and I've talked personally with hundreds of people who literally went from having zero to millions. I've had the opportunity to talk one-on-one, asking personal questions about how they got started, even watching them in operation.

The truth is that most are down-to-earth people, just like you and me, who want to provide a good life for their families and leave something of value when they're gone.

On top of my personal experience with people who are well off, I've conducted ground-breaking surveys of more than 3,000 Americans. I looked at the wealthy to see if, in fact, my theory was right. Then I talked to working Americans to see what is holding them back. I was amazed to find that even millionaires (people with a net worth of at least $1 million, not including their primary residence) had fears to overcome. In fact, the overwhelming majority said they had to step outside their "Comfort Zones" to become wealthy— something they had in common with everyone else.

My research confirmed my unique concept that financially successful people used the principles I describe in this book to overcome their fears, move beyond their current Comfort Zones, and use what's right in front of them to enter the Millionaire Zone.

How do I know my system works? I've helped thousands of Americans as CEO of Openshaw's Family Financial Network, founder of themillionairezone.com, AOL's Family Financial Editor, and host of "Winning Advice" on ABC Radio. As a money expert on a variety of TV shows, including *Dr. Phil, Oprah, Good Morning America*, the *CBS Early Show*, and NBC's *Nightly News*, I've seen the difference my strategies have made in people's lives.

Whether you have money or not, whether you are entrepreneurial or not, the information in the pages that follow will make a huge difference in your life.

Looking for Help in All the Wrong Places

Why haven't you built the kind of wealth you'd like to have? What's stopping you from moving forward?

If you've been looking for help, good luck. There are hundreds of books and articles out there by money experts all telling you how to get rich. I know, I've read a lot of them. So why haven't they worked for you?

There's a problem with them. They all depend on you, and you alone, to do the work. To do the thinking. To do the planning. To do the saving. Whatever. And what's the result? Shocking disclosure: You end up feeling alone. Confused. Anxious. Even with the simplest set of directions, if you're flying solo, it's going to be a long trip.

The truth is, to try to hit the Millionaire Zone when all the burden is on you alone is incredibly difficult, if not impossible.

But the good news is, you've found this book. If you've never bought a book about making money or changing your life, or you've read them all, this is what you've been looking for and all you'll need.

I am going to change the way you look at your life. Not by showing you something you don't know, but by showing you something you know very well. I will be showing you the way to the Millionaire Zone by *reintroducing* you to people, places, and resources that are already familiar, but in a context that will be quite different than anything you've seen. I know it will give you confidence, not uncertainty; courage, not fear.

Believe me, if I had known when I started my first company what I'm going to teach you here, my life would have been much, much easier, and a lot more fun.

What You Get with *The Millionaire Zone*

✦ **Free Millionaire Zone Profile** to help set you on the right path to wealth
Through this extensive questionnaire, I will help you determine what your strengths and weaknesses are when it comes to reaching the Millionaire Zone. After answering these 50 key questions related to the four primary factors that you need to consider (personality, financial, risk, and time), I'll give you instructions on what you need to do to get moving on your path to wealth.

✦ **30-Day Getting Started Program**
This step-by-step guide provides concrete actions you should take—broken down into easy-to-accomplish daily activities to get you moving toward the Millionaire Zone. By the time you're done with the 30-day program, you'll have generated specific ideas for tapping into the people, places, and resources around you to launch into the Millionaire Zone.

I Am on a Mission

I've been there, right where you are today. When I was five years old, my mother divorced. Three years later, I was taking care of my two younger brothers while Mom was working two full-time jobs as a waitress to support us. By the age of twelve, figuring it was *all up to me,* I became absolutely driven to make it financially, to be independent. My first real job was as a maid at the Don Carlos Motel in Dana Point, California. I was fourteen, and I spent years on that path of dedicated self-reliance, convinced that the only way I'd succeed was on my own pure grit.

Later, as an adult, I worked in corporate America. As I watched merger after merger around me, I realized that, for me, it wasn't the path to a seven-figure fortune. Too much was out of my control. If I was going to work my butt off, then I wanted the upward potential of unlimited rewards.

I've also seen friends struggle through job losses, divorces, and other life-changing events, not to mention the incessant demands of work and parenthood. It seemed like they were on a treadmill they couldn't get off.

And when I first started as a financial commentator for CBS-TV in Los Angeles, I'll never forget the letters I received from working Americans. They were writing to reach out for help because—lo and behold—retirement was upon them and they had no money. Talk about scary. I responded as best I could, giving them information and pointing them to solutions. Their follow-up letters, saying that my advice had made a big difference, energized me to keep fighting for everyone's financial lives.

But it all hit home with the experiences my own parents faced when I was starting out in my career. My stepfather, one of the most honest, hard-working, law-abiding citizens I know, found himself out of work with no savings after suffering a debilitating stroke.

I'll never forget the day when he told me, as I sat across the table from him at our favorite diner, "I'll just take out a loan to cover the bills."

"No way!" I said, "You'll just dig yourself into a hole. The medical bills alone are $1,000 a month! Look, I've got a better idea. I may not be the easiest person to live with, but let me move back in with you and Mom. I'll help you make ends meet with the money I'm saving by not paying rent. At least until you get back on your feet."

Luckily, I was working full-time and my job happened to be

located near my parents. In the end, Dad ultimately got a good job—not so easy today for someone in his sixties—and despite having to make some tough financial choices, they took back their lives.

But to this day, the story is still not a perfect one. Like many working people, my parents continue to watch their medical bills eat up a big chunk of their income. And as far as an easy retirement goes, well . . . there's no real safety net and therefore no obvious alternatives. At least, not under the conventional system.

Since then, I've seen so many individuals trying to get ahead, but just not able to make it happen. Worse, I've seen people—too many people—not able to take advantage of the opportunities staring them straight in the face, not able to achieve their dreams. *My dream, with this book, is to change all that.*

You Are Not Alone

So how do millionaires get over their fears, and plow ahead to make their financial dreams a reality? What separates them from everyone else?

Like everyone else, Laura had been going it alone. I could truly understand her pain . . . and her fears. Whether you're single or married, younger or older, at home or in corporate America, no matter how hard you try or which system you use, you feel like a tightrope walker—without the net. Truth is, there *is* no safety net today. They've all but disappeared.

What, then, did these millionaires do differently?

Perhaps you, in your own experiences with successful people, have sensed a difference in the way they operate, in how they get things done. Hasn't it struck you how connected they are, how extensive their networks are? But being in the Millionaire Zone is more than good networking. Much, much more.

What I have finally realized is that these people don't go it alone. They use a web of interconnecting assets—the people, places, and resources they know best—to get them where they want to go.

By using this web, or LifeNet as I call it, they are able to work within their Comfort Zone and move forward effectively, not stuck in the do-it-yourself paradigm. They manage to get all the elements of their LifeNet to work together as a unit to help them achieve their goals. In their quest for a better life, they are truly not alone.

The Millionaire Zone is not a place or a net-worth statement. It is where very successful people, and all their resources, come together. It is a state of being where all your family, friends, colleagues—every member of your LifeNet—function together every day, seamlessly, to help build your business, your career, your wealth.

Why is it that millionaires always seem to know the right person to call to get something done? Why do those contacts always respond so quickly and effectively? How do millionaires know how to bring all those elements together and always seem able to coordinate them to deliver the goods? And why are they ultimately able to make more money than everyone else?

That's what I'm going to teach you in the pages that follow.

THE MILLIONAIRE ZONE:
Seven Winning Steps
to a Seven-Figure Fortune

The Millionaire Myth

You could say rugged individualism is the American way. It's the story we see all around us. It's the ethic behind Hollywood's power hitters, and it's behind the Horatio Alger mantra that, no matter what, we can all pull ourselves up by our own bootstraps. We're told all we have to do is buckle down, work hard, and eventually we'll succeed.

That's the story we're told—and it's the story we believe when we read about John D. Rockefeller, Henry Ford, Bill Gates, Warren Buffett, and a few women like Mary Kay, Martha Stewart, and Oprah, or any of the millionaires and billionaires whose stories surround us on television and in magazines.

The usual line is that these people struggled against terrific odds, alone against the world. They achieved the American dream and became extremely wealthy because they were extraordinary individuals. To make it in this world, we're told, you've got to make things happen *on your own*. We've all been taught that the way to make money is through individualism. To get ahead, you have to do it on your own, it's all up to you.

There's only one problem with this story: It's not true. The financially successful people you see all around you did not get there on their own.

I'm going to tell you in this book exactly how people in the Millionaire Zone got there. And, I'll tell you exactly how to make this solution work for you, just like the real-life stories you'll read.

After years of working with, talking to, and observing very wealthy individuals, I began to see a common theme. *Successful people don't get there alone.* That's the revolutionary message behind this book.

There are thousands of theories espousing the next great way to get rich, but you have to execute them on your own. You have to get into real estate on your own, you have to day-trade on your own, you have to do X or Y or Z on your own. It's always all on your shoulders. The experts say, "Here's how, now go out and get 'em!" That's very simplistic, and of little real value. You either get it or you don't. Good luck!

The typical working American rarely achieves anything substantial by going it alone. We're too busy with our kids, dragged down by our jobs, fearful of the risk, unsure of what to do, or confused. Sound familiar to you? You're not alone. According to my research, 53% of Americans say they'd like to supplement their income or start their own business but feel anxious about venturing out on their own.

The Rules of the Game Have Changed

Even when I attended business school, the fundamental philosophy seemed to be to just go out, find a job, and make money. That usually meant to go work for someone else.

But these days, that's dicey advice. Who wants to be at the mercy of a company for the rest of their working lives when jobs are being sent overseas, mergers and buyouts are wreaking havoc with employees' lives, and "right-sizing" (i.e., slashing jobs) is the name of the game?

It's harder than ever to get ahead now that the loyalty bond between employer and employee that was there during our parents' generation has evaporated—the victim of a global economy, the technological revolution, disappearance of pensions, and corporate America's never-ending search for higher quarterly earnings.

Companies such as United Airlines and Bethlehem Steel, which promised generous pensions and medical benefits in retirement to the workers who were loyal to them for decades, have since reneged on those promises.

These days, even financially healthy companies such as IBM and Verizon are freezing their pensions, meaning that workers will end up with far fewer guaranteed benefits than they were expecting. Meanwhile, half of American workers don't have any kind of pension at all, and most of the rest are relying on a 401(k) plan—the very epitome of go-it-alone.

With a traditional pension your benefits are guaranteed, but with a 401(k) all the risk is on the individual to save enough (your employer's matching contributions notwithstanding), make the right investment choices, and figure out how to make your nest egg last through your retirement. And, trust me, even if you did save through your 401(k) during your career, chances are you wouldn't be close to having what you need for retirement: A 32-year-old making $30,000 a year would only have about $102,750 at the age of 67, assuming he or she contributed 3% of their salary to a 401(k) and received a company match of 1.5%, according to Vanguard. So much for the golden years.

Here's another sign that it's only getting harder to get to the Millionaire Zone, especially if you're trying to do it on salary alone: The inflation-adjusted income of the median household in 2004 was 3.8% *lower* than in 1999, according to the Economic Policy Institute's analysis of census data.

➤ FAST FACTS: Americans at Risk: A Decade of Decline

	Then	Now
Wage growth adjusted for inflation[1]	0.5%	–1.3%
Personal savings rate[2]	4%	–1.7%
Americans facing retirement risk[3]	38%	43%
Workers covered by a pension[4]	50%	22%

Sources:
1. Bureau of Labor Statistics, June 1996 and May 2006.
2. Dept. of Commerce, 1996 and 2006.
3. Center for Retirement Research at Boston College, 1995 and 2004, representing the percentage of Americans who will not be able to maintain their standard of living during retirement.
4. Bureau of Labor Statistics, based on medium and large private employers, 1987 and 2005.

The reality of our wages situation, combined with disappearing pensions, higher college costs, and rising health-care costs, is hitting our savings rate hard: Personal savings has been running *negative* for 16 straight months. How do you get a negative savings rate? By borrowing money or selling assets to support your spending habits.

Now take a look at the returns on your own money. How have you done? Have you handled your savings like millions of others, leaving it in a checking or savings account at, maybe, 3%? Are you among those who, even if you've stashed money aside through your 401(k), didn't carefully choose which funds you're invested in? Is what you're stashing in your retirement account going to get you through retirement? Get your kid to college? Enable you to start that nonprofit you always dreamed of?

Obviously it's important to keep some money invested in low-risk, low-return investments. You want a balanced portfolio and you want to invest according to your risk tolerance. But you also need to consider your future, and decide whether moving yourself closer to the Millionaire Zone requires taking some steps toward higher returns.

➤ FAST FACTS: Will Your Money Make You Rich?

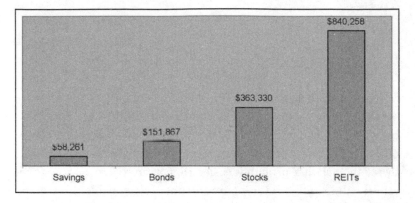

What $10,000 invested 30 years ago would be worth today

Sources: Ibbotson Associates, based on U.S. 30-Day T-Bill Index, U.S. Long-Term Government Bond Index, the S&P 500 Index, and the FTSE-NAREIT Equity Index, 1975–2005. REITs, which stands for real-estate investment trusts, invest in income-generating commercial real estate.

A Wake-Up Call

Yes, these statistics are depressing. But rather than letting these numbers beat you into submission, consider them a wake-up call. The American dream is still very much attainable. The impact of the economic dislocation our society has undergone in the last twenty years just means we need to change the rules of the game, so that the dream remains ours.

What about turning $5,000 into $1 million? Many have done it, and you'll hear some of their stories in this book.

My experience is that average working Americans are severely disadvantaged. Even if they've dedicated 20 or 30 years of their life to one company, it's unlikely they'll ever create a seven-figure fortune. And many of them seem to know it: 50% of employed Americans surveyed for this book said they are "very" or "somewhat" pessimistic that they will make a lot of money in their lifetime. For most of us, to achieve real financial independence, the only way up is out!

The New Millionaires

The first key to becoming a millionaire is to believe it's possible for you. Guess what—it is! Despite all the hurdles we've just discussed that society and corporate America have thrown in front of us in the last few decades, there is plenty of good news out there. In fact, it's probably easier than ever to create your own venture and reach a seven-figure fortune. Just consider how many people do it today.

➤ FAST FACTS: Millionaires on the Rise

	1997	1998	1999	2000	2001	2002	2003	2004	2005
Millionaires (000's)	1,800	1,840	2,170	2,180	2,220	2,141	2,472	2,715	2,901
Growth (%)		2.2%	17.9%	0.5%	1.8%	-3.6%	15.5%	9.8%	6.9%

Source: Cap Gemini & Merrill Lynch. Growth represents increase from the previous year.

Why is it that so many more people are millionaires today? Well, thanks to inflation, a million dollars is worth less in relative terms than it was 50 or 100 years ago. But more people are millionaires because the way we make money these days is fundamentally different than it was when Henry Ford started making the cars that fueled his fortune.

For Ford, Carnegie, Rockefeller, and other millionaires of the early part of the twentieth century, creating wealth was all about controlling resources, such as oil, railroads, or manufacturing. Such individuals tended to be older, experienced men of business.

These days, people become millionaires thanks to three important trends. First, the vast advancements in technology mean that today the world truly is flat. Technology allows us to operate globally. Thanks to the Internet, a person in the U.S. can do business in China, right from his garage in Hoboken. Plus, the Internet is teaching people skills they would never have gotten to learn just a few decades ago. Heck, you can do everything from taking a real-estate investment class in the comfort of your home to creating an ad for a product at 10 a.m. and knowing by noon if it's working. And those technological changes also mean the costs of entry are lower, giving the average person a greater chance of starting a business. You can hire someone overseas to build a Web site. You can find someone instantly on the Internet to help you design a brochure—at a cost you negotiate, based on your online research.

Second, entrepreneurialism is celebrated. A young person fresh out of college, a high school dropout, retirees—anyone!—can turn an idea into a product or service. Open up the business section of any newspaper and you'll read all kinds of fascinating stories about hardworking individuals who have found a consumer need, or created one. YouTube, anyone?

Third, the rise of direct selling has opened up the door to building wealth for many ordinary Americans. More people with good ideas can now go straight to the consumer, often online. They've built entire businesses that way. We see more one-on-one marketing because technology allows it, and people are no longer hampered by the myth that only established companies can sell goods.

The Myth about Saving

If this chapter does nothing else, it should change your view about success. While it may seem as if the chips are stacked against you, there are some fundamental advantages to the way the world is structured today that Henry Ford could never have imagined. You don't have to know the richest people, or have connections in government, or be absurdly lucky. These days you just need some good ideas (and my strategy can help with those too!) and you need your LifeNet.

But before we delve into how to use your LifeNet to get ahead, I want to focus for a moment on another myth. It's the personal-finance solution de jour. Namely, that scrimping and saving is the only way to get ahead. Not only are we supposed to work harder than ever, relying solely on ourselves, we're also told to cut out the lattes, drive an old car, eliminate magazine subscriptions, and eat in every night.

These are not bad ideas. Pushing ourselves to work harder and being prudent when it comes to spending are certainly important elements to being successful. In this book, you'll meet people who are making seven-figure fortunes, and you can bet that none of them got there by slacking off or by going deep into debt to buy the latest fashions or brand-new luxury cars. I'm certainly not pooh-poohing thrift as a personal virtue. But I'm proud of the fact that I buy most of my clothes at 30% off or more. Even famed personal virtue investor Warren Buffett has lived in the same house in Omaha for the last 30 years and shops at discount stores. And many successful entrepreneurs have made a dollar go a long way in their businesses.

But in these pages, instead of focusing on ways to cut back, we'll target the income-producing side of the equation, and how people can become millionaires by using the LifeNet strategies I'll outline.

There's no doubt in my mind that hard work is the cornerstone of success. It's also true that you're not going to get anywhere by spending all your money on things you don't need. Saving is important. And the more debt you carry, the longer it's going to take you to dig out to financial freedom.

But I just don't believe you're going to make your first million by giving up that $3 latte every day for the rest of your life. I would argue focusing on pennies alone will doom you to failure. At some point, as with a failed diet, you're going to break down and buy the coffee, go out to a lavish meal, buy something you don't need—and then you'll feel really guilty about it. Often as not, that guilt makes us feel so bad we give up trying to save altogether, figuring financial success just isn't for us.

I've got a better idea. Rather than relying solely on yourself, on scrimping and saving to get ahead, why not start tapping into the people and resources that are all around you to turn your passion into profits?

So Here's the Secret

It isn't that America's storybook millionaires and billionaires made all that money on their own. It's just that the public traditionally perceives those fortunes having been built as solo endeavors. One name gets all the credit. The media always likes to trumpet the accomplishments of the individual because it's more dramatic and more consistent with our hero-worshipping culture.

The real story is a lot more complex and less dramatic. In fact, those millionaires and billionaires didn't do it alone. They had help, and plenty of it. Some autobiographies may even acknowledge that fact, but the critical reviews never pick up on it, or never connect the dots into a theory the way *The Millionaire Zone* does. I am going to show you that, despite popular perception, the financial moguls past and present—and thousands of others—did not get rich following the individualistic, go-it-alone approach.

The "I" Problem

Trying to do everything yourself leads to a cascade of negative events. It looks like this:

Individualism ➤ Isolation ➤ Inactivity

Let's look at each more closely.

Individualism

We've talked a lot about how our culture is steeped in individualism. The idea that we have to get ahead on our own grit is an idea that pervades our entire world, whether we're watching television, reading a book or the newspaper, or talking to friends or family.

Take a really mundane example. Think about the last time you could have used a hand emptying your garage or cleaning your house. Did you ask friends and family (other than your spouse) to help you out? I'm guessing the answer is no. But wouldn't you have gotten the job done in half the time if you had?

We're so used to the idea that everything we do in our lives is up to us that we usually don't even consider the kinds of resources and talents our family, friends, and acquaintances can bring to any of our endeavors. In *The Adventures of Tom Sawyer*, Mark Twain's hero is given the job by his aunt Polly of whitewashing the picket fence. By pretending that only very gifted artisans could be entrusted with such a delicate task, Tom cleverly induces his friends—in exchange for numerous gifts—to take over his whitewashing duties. Before long, he is relaxing under the shade of a big old tree, and his friends had given the fence three coats of whitewash. A perfect example of using your LifeNet!

Now let's look at our finances. Ask yourself why you haven't achieved the kind of wealth you'd like. Below I've listed some of the most common reasons people give for their inability to get ahead financially. Do any apply to you?

- I don't have enough time.
- I have too much debt.
- I'm afraid of running out of money.
- I'm confused about where to start.
- I'm worried about the loss of prestige—I have a good job now!

- I can't risk being unable to support my family.
- I'm the only breadwinner.
- I'm too old to start a business.
- I'm too young to start a business.
- I'm interested in too many things—I wouldn't know where to begin.
- I don't have enough education or training.
- I've tried starting a business—and failed.
- I'd need a lot of money to start, and there's no way I'd get a loan from a bank.
- I've been turned down once before and don't have the courage to start again.
- I need to come up with a good idea.

Do any of these excuses sound familiar? All are normal fears that many of us have felt at one time or another, even those who are already in the Millionaire Zone. Unfortunately, if you adopt just one of those beliefs, it's enough to stop you in your tracks, without ever trying to turn your passions into profits. Of course, doing it all on your own *is* daunting. It makes sense that you'd be worried!

The beauty of the LifeNet approach is that you don't have to do it all on your own. The more you share these concerns with the people around you—your family, your friends, and your community—the more likely it is you'll find solutions. These solutions will soon start to stare you in the face, once you take the necessary step of including your family, friends, and community in your dreams.

Isolation

The most immediate by-product of our focus on individualism and the do-it-yourself myth of wealth-building is that you feel isolated. No surprise there. After all, you're doing this on your own! But if creating a business or starting a venture is supposed to be so empowering, why are you feeling so lousy?

I remember sitting in business school some years ago and feeling like something was wrong. Every course seemed designed for someone who was part of a larger organization. Excuse me, but if I'm going to work my butt off, I want the upside potential to be unlimited. Yet going it alone seemed incredibly daunting. There were not many classes teaching how to make that happen, though it's changed since then. I had to learn it the hard way.

You've heard of the saying "It's lonely at the top"? Well, it's not only lonely when you're alone, it also can be stressful and debilitating. I remember building my first financial services company, just before the tech meltdown in 2000. There were days when I needed to bounce an idea off someone else, and there were days when I just needed to know that someone was there, listening. When I didn't have that, my confidence dropped and my excitement diminished. Isolation, plain and simple, causes us to lose perspective and confidence. Over the years, I found out the hard way—and saw the same thing happen to others—that if you start out trying to get to this pinnacle of achievement completely on your own, you will become frustrated, fearful, and angry.

The beauty of my path to wealth is that you are not isolated. You can get to that summit with the help of your LifeNet resources—and you'll never again feel the anxiety and the loss of confidence of going it alone.

Inactivity

Feeling isolated and alone in the pursuit of your dream usually triggers feelings of inadequacy and helplessness. Then, when hurdles or obstacles arise, the tendency is to freeze up and stop moving forward. That's exactly how my friend in the TV audience described her feelings in the Introduction of this book. What's the inevitable next step? We quit.

This inactivity reveals itself in a variety of ways. Do you recognize any of these feelings or situations?

- You're too uncertain to reach out for help.
- You don't take even the smallest risks, when you know in your gut they'll pay off.
- You keep thinking negative thoughts: "*I can't do this*," "*I'm going to fail.*"
- You have an idea for turning a passion into a profitable venture, but you don't think it's good enough.
- You want to start, but don't know where to begin.
- You know you need to learn more before diving in, but you don't know where to get that knowledge.

The result is that we don't move forward financially in ways that are possible, ways that are right before us:

- You let money sit in a checking account rather than investing it.
- You have a subscription to *Entrepreneur* magazine and you haven't read it in six months.
- You purchased software to manage your expenses but you've never opened the package.
- Your daughter bought you a book on Warren Buffett's investing philosophy and you haven't gotten past the first page.

The "S" Solution

The cumulative effect of these feelings is that the goals that really matter to you—the future that you feel so passionate about—begin to look unachievable. You lose confidence and the next thing you know you're settling. Believe me, I know.

But if you keep reading, you'll discover that, with your LifeNet, you don't ever get into that cycle of the "the 'I' problem." That's because you're working within a framework—a kind of safety net—that leaves you feeling *supported* instead of alone, *surrounded* by resources instead of isolated, and *sure of yourself* rather than inactive, which looks like this:

Supported ➤ Surrounded ➤ Sure of Yourself

The End Zone

We've seen in this chapter that going it alone is not the right way to go about creating wealth. So what now? What do you do with this information? Now comes the part where you stand up tall, look yourself in the mirror, and say: "I have a responsibility to both myself and my family to wake up, to pay attention to the voice inside me that is saying 'I can do better'—and to do something about it!"

If you're tired of not reaching your financial goals, and you're ready to make a change, read on! In the next chapter, I show you how to get started with my new, better way: the LifeNet way.

My Big Fat Secret

Do you believe that the real winners in society are go-it-alone go-getters? *Should* you believe it? I'm here to tell you: No! It's simply not true. It's not the way success happens in real life. Deep down, you and I both know that to get to the place we really want to be financially, to make our dreams come true, we can't do it alone.

When I was building my first company, a senior executive of a big accounting firm (who later became involved in buying my company), said to me, "You didn't really build it alone. You weren't *really* by yourself." His comment angered me because I *felt* alone, especially in the early days.

I told him, "Yes I was! I had a friend review legal documents in the earliest days, but otherwise it really *was* just me trying to build a network of financial advisers and making this whole thing happen." I could see his point, though: Anyone trying to do it herself is crazy! And as I think back on those days, I can see the weight I put on my shoulders by trying to do it by myself. It's so difficult for anyone going it alone that the odds of success are vastly diminished.

Take a look at the people who've made it in this world: They're not alone. They've got friends, family, acquaintances, and you can bet their support system—their LifeNet—helped turn them into the success stories they are today. In fact, my research data show that high-net-worth Americans readily rely on their LifeNet to get ahead.

I'm not talking about cash. Your LifeNet is more than simply a way to fund your path to success. No, your LifeNet is much, much more than that.

> Your LifeNet is your life's network of familiar things—people, places, and resources—that you tap into to build your net worth and provide your family's safety net.

Notice I said *familiar* things. I'm not suggesting you start throwing yourself at strangers and asking them for help (at least, not yet). I'm also not suggesting you become someone you're not. Instead, this book is all about tapping the resources you've got all around you, right now.

My good friend Maryanne—I've known her since second grade—is a perfect example. Her husband is 60, and she's determined that he won't have to work past 70. The problem is, their retirement accounts aren't beefy enough, at this point, for him to stop working for a good while past 70.

So 41-year-old Maryanne started thinking about her strengths, about the things she really likes to do in life. She wondered whether her passion for feeding her family healthy foods might translate into an ability to sell nutritional supplements and other health-care products. She knew a neighbor—another stay-at-home mom—who was earning thousands of dollars a month doing just that. So she tapped her LifeNet to find out more. She talked to her family and friends about her idea and got the feedback and the support she needed to start developing a plan.

Let's see how Maryanne used her LifeNet to get things going:

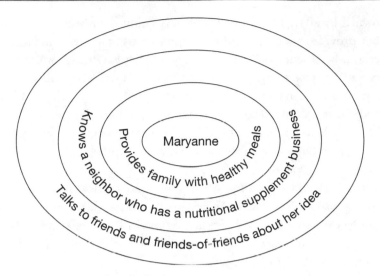

Figure 1.   Maryanne's LifeNet

YouTube Founders Tap Into Their LifeNets

But your LifeNet is more than just one good friend, or your supportive wife or husband. Take a look at Steve Chen and Chad Hurley, founders of the online video company YouTube, who sold it for almost $1.7 billion in less than two years: two names in the world of online business who were virtually unknown just months ago—and two people who could not have built YouTube alone. In fact, from the very beginning, these two friends were using their LifeNets and leveraging off each other's skills and support to fulfill their dream.

It all started out with a very simple idea: They wanted to get their home videos to their friends or whoever wanted to see them. Pretty soon, the idea of reaching out from their LifeNet to yours caught like wildfire and grew to more than 100 million videos being viewed at YouTube.com *every day.*

And there were others in their LifeNets, too. For instance, both Chen and Hurley were part of a whole network of friends developed during their days working at PayPal, the online payment system owned by eBay. These friends not only enjoyed barbecues together, but provided support, feedback, connections, and even funding for each other's ventures, long after they had left PayPal, according to a *New York Times* article entitled "It Pays to Have Pals in Silicon Valley." Can you imagine YouTube's birth without the help of Chen and Hurley's LifeNets? It just would not have happened. Who knows where Chen and Hurley might have ended up if they didn't have their LifeNets to provide support and to help them get their idea off the ground.

And it's not only Steve Chen and Chad Hurley. Based on my survey of high-net-worth Americans, it's clear that tapping one's LifeNet is part and parcel of reaching the Millionaire Zone. Take a look, on the following page, at how those in the Millionaire Zone used their LifeNet to get there.

Among those with a net worth of $1 million or more, 50% said business contacts and relationships had a "big" or "some" impact on their financial success, followed by family and friends. Note that even neighbors, clubs, and your local government can have a significant impact on your success, as they did with these millionaires.

Wealthy Americans Know the Power of LifeNet

Here's more proof that your LifeNet is key to reaching the Millionaire Zone. According to my survey research, more than one-third of high-net-worth individuals say they should have focused more strongly on their LifeNets.

Even more telling, my research shows that those in the Millionaire Zone are more likely to say they relied on their LifeNet than those who are not yet in the Millionaire Zone. These people are strongly aware that their LifeNet is the key to their success.

If you compare two high-net-worth groups—both of which have investable assets of at least $500,000, but the people in one group have a net worth of $1 million or more while those in the other

➤ FAST FACTS: How Those in the Millionaire Zone Used Their LifeNet

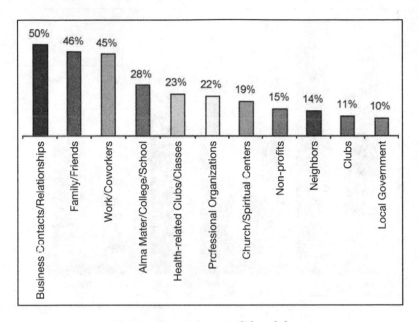

**How strong an impact did each have
on becoming a millionaire?**

Source: The Spectrem Group for Jennifer Openshaw
Note: Percentages refer to answers citing "big" or "some" impact

group are not yet millionaires—you will find that those who are in the Millionaire Zone say they used their LifeNet to a greater extent.

For example, among those in the Zone, 64% said they received introductions to others while only 53% of those not yet in the Zone said they benefited from introductions. Those in the Zone consistently said they benefited—more than was reported by those not in the Zone—through information, business partnerships, and advice as well as emotional, financial, and practical support (such as reviewing a business plan).

➤ **FAST FACTS:** Those in the Millionaire Zone Relied on Their LifeNets More Than Those Not in the Zone

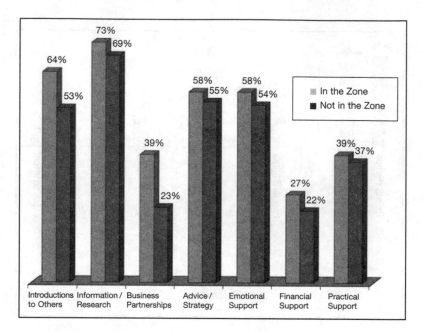

Source: The Spectrem Group for Jennifer Openshaw

Many Roads, One Destination

Okay. You're getting a feel for what I mean when I say LifeNet. But you're wondering how all of this *works*, and how you can use this thing I call your LifeNet to reach your financial goals.

I've got seven key strategies for you to follow, outlined below and detailed in the subsequent chapters. I'm going to lay out a step-by-step plan for understanding the who, what, and how of the resources you can access to move to a new financial level.

But before I introduce you to my seven key strategies, I want to mention one thing: There is no one right way to financial success. Let me clarify. You do need to rely on my seven key strategies—my

LifeNet approach—to reach your financial goals, but you can apply my approach to any number of paths to get you to the Millionaire Zone.

For instance, you could start your own home-based business, or maybe you want to keep your full-time job but do some freelance or consulting work, or start investing in real estate on the side. Another path would be to become an independent consultant outside the home. Just check out the many ways those who are already in the Millionaire Zone have achieved their goals. We asked millionaires in what ways they primarily achieved financial success. As you can see below, many achieved their success not through just one path but through several routes, combining real estate with a business, for instance.

➤ **FAST FACTS: How Millionaires Got There**

Stock market or other investments	65%
Paid employment working for someone else	58%
Real estate	54%
Independent consultant/contractor	37%
Received inheritance of more than $50,000	30%
Started self-funded business outside the home	29%
Started home-based business	17%
Partnered with existing company (franchise/marketing/distributor)	14%
Started business funded by others	12%
Invented product	3%

Source: The Spectrem Group for Jennifer Openshaw

Your Path to the Millionaire Zone

We've looked at some of the ways millionaires have reached the Zone. How about you? Not every path to the Zone is for everyone. That's why I created the Millionaire Zone Profile (outlined in Chapter 12) to help people like you figure out which path to the Millionaire Zone is right for them.

If you're like most people, you fall into at least one of three groups: You're working for someone else as an employee; you're working for yourself as an entrepreneur, sole proprietor, or business owner; or you're investing your money into other people's ventures. It looks like this:

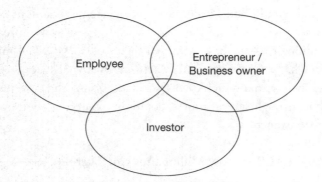

Figure 2.   Which One Are You?

A Bigger Paycheck

I showed you in Chapter 1 why getting a paycheck alone usually isn't enough to make you rich. But you may not be ready yet to start your own venture. That's okay. There are ways to use your LifeNet to help move you up the corporate ladder and into a position of greater wealth. Did you know that surveys show that the most common way to get hired is through a referral? That's one way your LifeNet can make a difference: You can tap your LifeNet to move into a higher-paying position. Or, you might use your LifeNet to start generating income on the side by marketing someone else's products, or perhaps by opening up a franchise that a family member manages. Or you could take that great idea you've had and license it to someone who can take it to the next level while you collect some of the revenue it earns, as a colleague of mine has done literally hundreds of times. And still another option is to use the principles in this book to invest better—earning far more than you would by simply plunking your savings into some checking account or even mutual fund. My Millionaire Zone Profile will help you figure it out.

A Better Investor—Your Own Adviser

Sadly, consumers lose $30 billion to $50 billion annually by failing to properly invest the $1 trillion they leave in low-yielding savings accounts, according to research conducted by the nonprofit advocacy group Consumer Federation of America. Are you one of those people? If so, we're going to change that! Now, I understand the dilemma. Investing takes time and you're busy. Maybe you've thought of getting a financial adviser but you can't find one you trust. Or maybe you're like others who have come to me saying, "Jennifer, I don't have anywhere near $1 million and no adviser will talk to me without *at least* that much—how can I make my money grow?"

What's your alternative? How about connecting with others— those in your LifeNet—and those available to you through www.themillionairezone.com? That's what Tiger 21 is all about. This group of high-net-worth individuals meets once a month to discuss their investments and other money-making strategies. By pooling their knowledge, members of Tiger 21 are able to get higher returns while paying lower investment fees.

➤ **FAST FACTS: Tiger 21 Takes Matters into Their Own Hands**

Tiger 21 (The Investment Group for Exceptional Returns in the 21st century) is a small but affluent group of like-minded CEOs, entrepreneurs, and others with at least $10 million in wealth. The group was formed because, as cofounder Michael Sonnenfeldt told *Business Week*: "I felt the advice I was getting was always tainted." I've heard the same from many Americans, whether they have $10 million or $10,000. Tiger 21 leverages off of one another's knowledge, sharing information on how to grow and preserve their wealth and bringing investment opportunities to the group. Results? Reginald Brack, former CEO of Time, Inc., had been a client of a top investment bank and, not surprisingly, was charged exorbitant fees. And the returns? They were flat, he says. But since joining Tiger 21, Reginald's returns are up 8% net of the group's $25,000 annual fee, he told *Business Week*. To find like-minded people with whom you can connect in a similar fashion, log onto www.themillionairezone.com.

Another example: The Young Presidents' Organization, an association of more than 10,000 young business leaders spanning a number of countries. Local chapters meet regularly to discuss the best business practices and investment strategies. If you talk to any young yet highly successful business owner, you're likely to hear "YPO" pop up in the conversation. These business owners often say that the problems they resolved—and avoided!—by meeting regularly with their local YPO have been crucial to their success.

Profit from a Big Idea

Finally, maybe you're the entrepreneur with ideas—maybe even a hobby—that you want to turn into profits. Or perhaps you're running your own business and want to take it to a higher level. That's what I primarily focus on in this book—helping you turn an idea, a project, a venture into a real money maker. Keep in mind that projects or ventures don't necessarily have to be those you start on your own, out of your house. They could be started at your employer's, putting you on the fast-track at that company or even allowing you to transition out and build a product or service your old employer uses! I'll show you how others did exactly that.

When you're using your LifeNet and truly operating in the Millionaire Zone, the people and places you know will bring you ideas, resources, even business. You will be "top of mind" for them. You will know you're in the Zone because people will come to you, just as you go to them. By using the strategies outlined in this book, you will find reaching the Millionaire Zone through your ideas not only less risky and less stressful, but in fact more gratifying and much more promising.

Now Let's Get Going

You can get to the Millionaire Zone whether you're an employee, investor, or entrepreneur. Now you need my seven key strategies to help get you there.

At the beginning of every chapter detailing these strategies, you'll meet someone who's already in the Millionaire Zone. I've talked to many others who are either in the Millionaire Zone or well on their way to reaching it, and you'll find their stories throughout the book. You will read in the words of these real-life "Zoners" how they all used their LifeNets to propel themselves into the Millionaire Zone.

Key 1: Wire Your LifeNet

The first key strategy is to figure out the people, places, and resources that make up your LifeNet. Don't rush through this step. I'm sure you can rattle some names off the top of your head, but you'll need to really think this through carefully. Your LifeNet is the heart of what you're going to use to propel your dreams forward. You'll continually come back to these people, places, and resources as, over time, you move ever closer to your goals.

Based on my research, it's clear that many regular Americans are willing to tap into their LifeNets but just don't know how yet: 56% of employed Americans said they'd be less fearful about starting their own business if they could learn how to take advantage of people and organizations for support.

Well, get ready to learn what you need to know! In the next chapter, you'll meet Desma Reid-Coleman, a divorced mother of four who's also a millionaire running three businesses. Desma could never have reached the Millionaire Zone without her LifeNet. Each of her companies was fueled by the various people, places, and resources that she already had at her fingertips. In fact, she developed two of her businesses based on ideas suggested by people in her LifeNet! She's a superb example of how to tap into the people, places, and resources you encounter in your everyday life as a means to achieving financial success.

Desma exemplifies how my Wire Your LifeNet strategy works. Her story shows that all you need to do is turn to your LifeNet to realize your dreams. Of course you need to be patient. You need to be prepared to spend some time getting from where you are now to where you want to be.

Impatient? Yes, most of us are. I know I am.

But when you hear the stories I'll detail in this book—the stories of people who went from day-to-day drudgery to realizing their dreams—you'll notice some common themes. One of those similarities is that they all tapped into their LifeNet. Another theme: Many of them developed a plan—often a five-year plan—for getting to where they wanted to be. In fact, having a plan may be vital to your success: 77% of millionaires say they developed a plan for making their current wealth. So be sure to spend some time with me in the next chapter detailing the whos and whats that make up your LifeNet. This is your road map for your future success.

Key 2: Redefine Your Comfort Zone

In Chapter 4, I'll let you in on a secret. Let me give you a hint now.

I've talked to a lot of regular people in my travels who've tried various strategies to create wealth. They read the latest "make-a-million" book and lap up the information with the best intentions of following the author's tips. They try for a while, they work very hard at it, yet they still fail. They just can't seem to put it to work in their own lives, or to sustain the strategy over time.

Why? Other wealth-building strategies push us into unknown territory, into trying things that really don't suit our natures. That's the wrong way to go about it. Why? *If we're out beyond our Comfort Zone, afraid of what's happening or what might happen, then the slightest obstacle will send us scurrying back to where we were before: that comfortable place we've inhabited for so long.*

I'm going to reposition your mind when it comes to fears and your Comfort Zone. I want you to think about making money in a way that makes you feel comfortable and confident, paving the way from the daily grind into the Millionaire Zone.

Over the years, I've learned that you can't reach your goals unless you feel secure about what you're doing. That is, stay within your Comfort Zone but take a fresh look at your everyday life, and see where you can refine it, a step at a time. Doesn't that thought alone make you feel better about making changes in your life? The trick is to figure out what your Comfort Zone is—what it is about your life that makes you feel secure and familiar—and then redefine it in a way that still feels comfortable but that moves you toward a seven-figure fortune.

This means taking baby steps, not seismic shifts, to something new, just like Mark Fitzgerald did. When he was in his thirties, working at a tech company that had just been bought out by another firm, Mark realized that his dream was to start his own business. But when he actually made that leap to entrepreneurship, it wasn't a huge leap. He made sure he had some customer contacts in place, and some savings in the bank. Plus, his first company was closely related to the firm he had worked for—he even started it with a coworker from that firm. In other words, he took small steps forward, first starting a company in an industry he knew well. Since then, he's started a number of successful ventures. His online shoe store currently enjoys annual revenue of about $25 million. Mark's story is a clear example of how to shift your Comfort Zone into new realms.

Key 3: Ready, Set . . . Home Zone

If you've failed until now to get where you want to be financially, it's easy to think that there's nothing in your life that could change your situation. You look around and think: *Here I am, making $45,000 a year. I have to change everything if I'm ever going to earn a seven-figure fortune.*

You might think you need to move to another city, earn an advanced degree, completely change your career—do anything, as long as it's 180 degrees away from whatever it is you're doing now.

That kind of thinking is a by-product of the good old myth of individualism our country so highly values. It's the notion that our own grit is the only thing that's going to get us from where we are to the attainment of our dreams.

Luckily, just because that attitude is prevalent doesn't mean it has to be that way. If it were, a lot of us would be failing instead of succeeding! The people you read about who've made their millions did not do it alone, and they often tapped the people and resources that were right in front of them.

Consider Wayne Finkel and his wife, Charlene Rios. Wayne's an auditor who spent years working at a midsize auditing firm keeping an eye on the books kept by some of the largest companies in this country. Wayne roots out fraud and corruption, and assures companies (and shareholders) that their accounting practices are solid. He worked for an expert in the field, but he kept seeing how he could do a much better job than some of the independent contractors his company hired during busy times. Now he runs his own multimillion-dollar company, with Charlene playing a vital role. He did it all by simply perceiving the demand that was staring him in the face while he went about his nine-to-five job.

Think of it this way: Knowledge is power, right? You wouldn't walk into an important meeting without having read up on your subject. Focusing on what I call your Home Zone—the people, places, and resources closest to you—is one way of leveraging the knowledge you already have. Rather than diving into completely unfamiliar territory, think about what you know well. That's going to be the place you start looking for your path to the Millionaire Zone.

Key 4: From Passions to Profits

If you do follow your bliss you put yourself on a kind of track that has been there all the while, waiting for you, and the life that you ought to be living is the one you are living. When you can see that, you begin to meet people who are in your field of bliss, and they open doors to you. I say, follow your bliss and don't be afraid, and doors will open where you didn't know they were going to be.

—Joseph Campbell, from the documentary *Joseph Campbell and the Power of Myth*, a series of interviews with Bill Moyers, 1988

Here's something that is *not* a secret: Doing what you love to do makes work not seem like work. Focusing on what you're passionate about (or following your bliss, as Joseph Campbell famously called it) is essential to getting motivated to take steps toward your financial success. Each one of the people profiled in this book truly gushes with enthusiasm over what he or she does. You can't start a business without that drive, nor can you propel your career forward without a lot of energy.

Let's not kid ourselves: Getting a venture off the ground takes enormous time and energy. So does constantly pushing your career to the next level within corporate America. In my survey of high-net-worth individuals, 82% said it took them more than five years to attain their financial success. You're going to need to love what you're doing to keep yourself going for the long haul, even when your biggest account calls to complain, or an employee asks for a raise, or scores of other issues arise, as they will with any venture or new project.

Of course, the whole point of this book is you're not doing it alone. When times get hard, you have your LifeNet for support. The success stories of the millionaires profiled in this book show how they all relied on others at various points in the game. You'll also see that they all have a passion for what they do.

What do I mean by passion? I suppose it's kind of an obsession. You love the product or the service you've developed so much that you feel people—your potential customers—won't be able to live without it.

Take Marnie Walker, for instance. When she was 17 years old, she fell down. A simple fall turned into eight years of being unable to walk normally. After that fall, her life turned upside down. She went from being captain of the cheerleading squad to finding that her friends would no longer talk to her. Yet years later she turned that experience into a $10 million bus transportation company serving special-needs kids. How, in her mid-thirties, did she go from a dull job at a phone company to growing a business that catapulted her into the Millionaire Zone? A passion for serving her customers well, including meeting with parents, working with school districts, and above all, making sure these kids could get to where they needed to go.

Tapping into your personal drivers is absolutely key to your success going forward. Of course, as you can guess, not all of our favorite hobbies are equally suited to transformation into dollars, so in Chapter 6—as well as in the 30-Day Getting Started Program in Chapter 12—you'll discover how to figure out which of your passions are most likely to become profit-making ventures.

Key 5: Make 'Em Want It

Once you've got a great idea for turning one of your passions into profits, does that mean you should run out to mortgage your home to finance it or leave your job? No.

In almost every instance, the best way to get going on your new idea is to make sure there's demand before sinking tons of money into it or making the jump. The more limited your audience, the more challenging it will be to grow your business and your personal wealth.

You know you need to step outside your Comfort Zone, to take *some* risks to move toward greater financial success. But that doesn't mean taking unnecessary risks, particularly the risk of overwhelming financial loss.

That's why it's essential to use your LifeNet to test your drivers—the particular passions that make you tick and propel you into your venture—against the demands of the real world.

How do you do that? Test demand for your product or service or idea using your LifeNet, and then create demand for it to ensure strong sales.

Erica Zohar, president of American Groove, is a great example of creating demand: She took $10,000 to get her venture off the ground. But before she had even a sewing machine for her business—now a multimillion-dollar high-end women's and children's sportswear company—she made sure someone would want to buy her clothes. She asked a tailor to make six sample clothing items and then asked her friends what they thought. She then flew to New York, shared a booth at a trade show with another clothing maker—and signed up $45,000 worth of orders. Rather than starting off by showing her fledgling work to store buyers, she shored up her confidence by finding out what the people around her liked to wear. Even now, when her company's incredibly successful, Erica *still* relies on her friends' insights and ideas about her clothes. She knows the power and value of her LifeNet to understand and create demand.

Key 6: Getting by Giving

Throughout this book you'll learn how critical your LifeNet is to your success. This web of people, places, and resources is vital to your reaching the Zone.

Your LifeNet plays such an important role in your life, including providing feedback, information, introductions, opportunities, and emotional support. It functions almost like your personal advisory board. You need to take special care of it.

It's as if your LifeNet is a breathing, functioning organism that requires care and feeding like any living thing. Learning how to do this takes practice, but if you follow my suggestions, you will have a vital LifeNet that will grow as you grow and be there when you need it.

Multimillionaire Bob Lorsch knows all about giving back to his

LifeNet. He attributes his success to doing just that. "One of the reasons that I have been successful is that in all my business endeavors—and as I go through my personal life—I look for ways to give," he says. "I look for ways to support people. I look for ways to inspire and motivate. Whether it's with money or with time, the more you put out, truly the more you get back."

Giving back to your LifeNet is essential to entering the Millionaire Zone, but there is a right and a wrong way to do it. And it's important to realize that the care and feeding of your LifeNet doesn't need to eat up hours of your time. There are easy ways you can support those around you. It won't take much effort on your part, but if you are truly in the Zone, that effort will reward you for years to come.

Key 7: Turn Rejection into Opportunity

Let's be honest: No matter how passionate and well prepared you are, there will be some people who reject your idea. It could be a close friend with whom you share your idea who tells you it's ridiculous. It could be 20 potential clients who all say "Thanks, but no thanks" when you try to pitch your product or service.

There is just no way everyone will be supportive of what you're trying to do. In fact, every successful entrepreneur has dozens of favorite stories of how often his ideas were turned down. *Harry Potter* author J. K. Rowling, a once-unemployed single mother whose books and movies have made her a billionaire, had her first manuscript rejected by 12 publishers! Rejection is just one of the hazards of moving into a new realm, a realm where you can realize greater financial success. For some of us, particularly women, this can be a tough strategy to implement. But it's within each and every one of us to turn rejection into opportunity.

Kevin DiCerbo has encountered plenty of rejection in trying to get his skin-care company off the ground. When he applied for a bank loan, dozens of banks said no. But he always ended those meetings with an important question: "I'd say, 'Okay, you can't do

it, but do you know someone else who could provide me a loan?' "
he says. "I met with about 50 people for financing or to ask for referrals. I finally found one out of those 50 bankers who believed in
me and my business and who wanted to increase their portfolio
even if it didn't include a real-estate component."

After all those rejections, Kevin got one yes—and that's all he
needed!

It wasn't easy, he says. "It's a roller-coaster ride. One day you
think you have a hot lead and the next day it completely dries up,"
he says. "But if you believe in the idea, you have to keep moving
forward."

The End Zone: The Power of LifeNet

As you'll see as you make your way through this book, self-made
millionaires consistently rely on their greatest asset, their LifeNet,
to move forward to greater financial success.

We *all* have LifeNets. No matter what your current financial
picture, you can get ahead if you focus on tapping your LifeNet using my seven key strategies.

Of course, there are some common myths about how people enter the Millionaire Zone. We'll debunk those in Chapter 11. And
we'll look at the problem of debt in Chapter 10. Many Americans
are struggling with debt, and that kind of money issue prevents
most of us from setting goals for the future. But it doesn't have to
be that way.

Finally, Chapter 12 gives you information about and access to
the Millonaire Zone Profile and my powerful 30-Day Getting
Started Program, so you can begin to put into practice the same
strategies that I and thousands of other millionaires before you
have used.

Are you ready to begin to enter the Millionaire Zone? Then
let's go!

Key 1: Wire Your LifeNet

To achieve your financial goal of entering the Millionaire Zone, you need to follow each of my seven key strategies. Each of the seven is equally important. You can't move forward to the place you deserve to be without them. But there's one strategy from which all of the other ones flow. That's why I'm starting with it. I call this strategy Wire Your LifeNet.

Remember, your LifeNet is the network of people, places, and resources you have around you, and it's essential to building your seven-figure fortune. This powerful LifeNet will be your path to building your own financial safety net. Consider this: 56% of working Americans surveyed for this book said they'd feel less fearful about starting their own business if they could learn how to take advantage of people and organizations for support. Meanwhile, 36% said they "feel alone" in their attempt to make more money. Well, I'm here to tell you there's no need to feel alone, and I'll explain exactly how to tap into your LifeNet to move toward your financial goals.

Before I go into more detail on what your LifeNet is and the benefits it will provide you, listen to Desma Reid-Coleman's story. I met Desma at a conference. She was talking to people about how to grow their businesses, and I was really struck by her canny insights into using who and what she knew to get ahead. Desma, a millionaire who is juggling three very different types of businesses, is a master at tapping into her LifeNet to move toward greater financial success.

CHAPTER CHECK-IN: How Desma Wired Her LifeNet

Desma was able to wire her LifeNet and thrive financially after a major life change by:

- Making a list of everyone and every organization she knew
- Involving friends, family, and community organizations, who reached out to their own LifeNet members on behalf of Desma, thus expanding Desma's own (and their) LifeNet
- Having her LifeNet members reach out to prospective customers to serve as an endorsement of Desma

Desma's Story

Like many people, an unexpected life change catapulted Desma into a new—and scary—financial situation: She went through a divorce. At the same time, her ex-husband's income dropped sharply, leaving it up to her to make up the gap in child support so that she and her four kids could maintain their standard of living.

After the divorce and her ex-husband's job change, "It was like, *whoa,*" Desma says. "Our situation went to hell in a handbasket."

What to do? Desma realized her best bet was to take advantage of her experience from a former job working in human resources for a large mechanical-engineering company to start her own human-resources consulting firm.

But how to start a business from scratch? As Desma soon learned, it's all about tapping into your LifeNet. Desma contacted all the people she had known through her previous job and her years of volunteer work.

"All the contacts I had built in that position and prior to that," she said, "I started calling people saying, 'I'm hanging my shingle out. Here's what I'm doing.'" She even put a brochure together on her new human-resource consulting company, which she calls Quality Professional Services.

Not only did she let everybody know she was in business, she also asked her LifeNet for help in setting up that business.

"I created my own list of family members, friends, committees, and other organizations—everyone I knew and everyone *they* knew—and we sent out personalized letters with the brochure letting them know about the business. And then we'd follow up after that. We didn't give up until we got an answer. At one time I had 11 people helping me out," she says.

Can you see how Desma was not only using her LifeNet but the LifeNets of her friends and family to get her business going? Can you see how this LifeNet she had created was also providing her with emotional support during a frightening transition? Desma's LifeNet had, in fact, become her safety net.

Even Desma's mother served as an important resource as Desma grew her businesses when later, in her resale clothing store, Desma discovered that $200 had been taken from the cash drawer. "I realized then I needed someone I could trust, to watch my back," says Desma. So she hired her mother—whose previous experience was working as a nurse for 40 years—for a two-day-a-week commitment. At first her mother was a bit reluctant, but she's now the store's full-time manager. "She loves doing the fashion merchandising stuff that she had never done before," says Desma. "It's what keeps her excited about life." See how Desma's mother has, in essence, served as a safety net while Desma, in turn, has provided her mother a new safety net and life-changing opportunity?

How Desma Reached the Millionaire Zone
- Generated three streams of revenue from ventures initiated and supported by her LifeNet
- Followed a "2-for-1" strategy of earning income while simultaneously engaging in LifeNet-expanding opportunities—for instance, while attending a business conference Desma would sell clothing from her hotel room, generating as much as $12,000 in a single day
- Gave her mother the responsibility of managing a business while providing her with a source of income and self-esteem
- Created a referral program for her resale clothing business so that those who play a direct role in selling clothes to new customers receive a 50% commission

Example from the Millionaire Zone
Phil Knight, founder, Nike
No. 31 on Forbes 400
Net worth: $6.9 billion
Key strategy: Wire your LifeNet

Phil Knight started his company based on one of his favorite activities: running. He'd been a track-and-field competitor in college, and continued running while attending business school at Stanford. While there, one of his class assignments was to write a plan for a small business based on something he knew, so Knight sketched out an idea for a company that would make running shoes. He ended up literally running with that plan—and wiring his LifeNet was a key factor in his success. After graduating from school, he went to Japan and met with the owner of a shoe manufacturing plant. The factory owner liked his business plan, so Knight turned to his father for some start-up funds to make a few sample shoes. Then he sent those samples to his old coach to get his ideas and input. His coach eventually became his business partner. And there you have it: His dad and his former coach are two key players in his LifeNet. Plus, as a former competitor and someone who still loved to run, Knight knew plenty of other people who also loved running. Those people became his first customers. Want yet another example of Knight wiring his LifeNet? You know the Nike "swoosh" logo, right? That was designed by an art student he knew. He reportedly bought that design from her for thirty-five dollars.

Let People Know Your Business

So right now you're probably thinking to yourself, *Well, Jennifer, if I'm supposed to wire my LifeNet, it sounds like I have to share the details of my private life. The last thing I want to do is tell my family and friends how much money I have . . . or, rather, don't have. And I'm not comfortable telling anyone about my dreams, my passions. I'm afraid they'll laugh or just not understand.*

We're not talking about how much money you do or don't have—we're talking about your project, your venture, or even your job and how to take you to the next level. We all know that sharing is a big issue, even when—especially when!—it's with your closest friends and family. And asking for help or even telling someone about your need for money to make your dream a reality can be embarrassing. But I've been there, too, and I've seen how the fear of letting others in can actually hold you back.

Let's ask ourselves, what are we afraid of? Is it that someone will share our private matters with others? Is it if we let them know we're not that financially successful now, they will think less of us? Is it that they will in some way abuse the information we've shared, that they won't treat it delicately? Is it that, by sharing your most intimate dreams and goals, you put extra pressure on yourself to succeed? (If no one knows I'm trying, no one knows if I fail.) There are ways to deal with these fears, and we'll get to them in a minute.

But first, remember this: If you don't open up and begin to trust in your LifeNet, you will go nowhere. How can someone help you if they don't know that you need help? In fact, opening up—sharing and learning—is essential to reaching the Millionaire Zone. And that's exactly what Desma experienced.

A funny thing will happen as you open up with those closest to you: You will get more support and insight than you ever imagined, the kind that will make you feel better and more confident about what you're venturing into. Rather than being laughed at or misunderstood, you may find that people are not only encouraging but may share with you *their* own passions and dreams. We all have them.

Look what happened with Desma: She let others know what she was taking on—a divorce and a new business—and what happened? Her support structure, her LifeNet, *wanted* to help her. By sharing and trusting, and positioning her transition as positive, she made it possible for her LifeNet to dive in.

QUICK TIP: Ask for Help

Asking for help with a job or venture can be difficult. Here are tips to make it easier:

- Keep it positive: Tell your story in a positive light. If you feel good about what you're doing, others will, too.
- Be direct: It's really the easiest way. Directly express your idea or need so your LifeNet member can be most helpful. Be honest and speak from the heart.
- Seek multiple opinions: Talk to many people. The more you do, the more practice you'll have opening up. Plus, you'll get a variety of perspectives that will help you make smarter decisions.
- Give, don't just take: Remember that this is a give-and-take process. Take the time to listen and ask how *you* can be helpful.

QUICK TIP: Help Your Family, Help Yourself

There are many benefits to hiring your kids or other family members, including:

- They gain valuable work experience that they can later leverage when entering the job market or making a career transition, avoiding a gap in their resume.
- Hiring your kids can serve as a tax deduction to you.
- Your teenager may be better skilled at tech chores that you hate to do, like backing up your computer or marketing on the Internet.
- Family members can begin saving under a tax-deferred 401(k) plan, thus keeping income the company would ordinarily pay out to employees within the family.

The "I'd Rather Not Bother People" Fear

Here's another common fear that pops up when people start thinking about turning to family, friends, and acquaintances for help: "Well, I don't want to bother anyone with my needs." Thanks to the individualistic culture in which we live, if you're feeling that way right about now, don't worry. You're not alone.

Instead of feeling as if you're being a burden to someone, think about all you've done—and will do in the future—for the people in your LifeNet. Here's how Desma looks at accessing her LifeNet: "I was always someone who had given back to the community or did dishes after a church event, so people would say 'if you ever need anything. . . .' So this was me calling in those chips," she says.

Others echo her thoughts. For instance, one of the key people in Desma's LifeNet is Edna Bell, a commissioner of Wayne County, Michigan, and member of the advisory board of the Joint Center for Sustainable Communities. Like Desma, Edna also runs three companies. And they're both part of each other's LifeNets. Edna has connected Desma to some of her biggest business deals.

Edna, too, says she wouldn't be where she is now without her LifeNet. "You can't make it without that. You have to have people around you with connections to be successful, to make the right moves at the right time," she says.

"I tell people to just sit down and write *who* you know and *what* you know, and then start connecting the dots—who can help you with what. Then, for the things you don't know, ask the people who *do* know." This is a really powerful concept and it's what wiring your LifeNet is all about.

Too often, Edna says, people are simply unwilling to ask for help from the people and organizations they know. "The average person is typically afraid to ask someone for something," she says. But that kind of fear will get you nowhere fast. "If you're going to make money, you can't be afraid of no," Edna says.

Of course, this isn't about *using* the people around you. Like any true relationship, there's a give-and-take, where you support your LifeNet just as it supports you.

"You want to come to the table with something," Desma says. "You don't want to come just begging. So be prepared to give as well as being needy, because folks don't want to be bothered with needy people. People get that all day and all night. Think about what can you do to make a difference," Desma says.

Keep in mind that wiring your LifeNet is not just chatting with your friends once in a while. You need to be persistent, and reach out to as many people and organizations as possible. When Desma was trying to get her human-resources business up and running, "it wasn't just a matter of sending someone a brochure, thinking you'll get the business. It was about following up," she says, "taking meetings, asking 'Can you give me a timeline?'" Desma talks to everyone she knows, plus people she meets along the way.

In fact, research shows that some of the most powerful connections we have are with people we don't know very well. Studies show that these relationships, ironically called weak ties, are sometimes more important than strong ties in landing a job. This is in part because these more distant acquaintances are likely to be spread out geographically and in different industries.

Relying on our most immediate circle of friends and family—what I call our Home Zone—is essential to becoming financially successful. It's just as important to reach out to those people we haven't spoken with in years. I keep track of everyone—for instance, someone I met on a plane three years ago—with the thought that he or she might be a key contact for my next venture.

➤ FAST FACTS: Weak Ties

Weak ties are more powerful than strong ties when it comes to landing a job, according to Mark Granovetter, a sociologist from Stanford University. That's because these ties to people we do not directly know are more diverse, spanning different towns, states, and even industries.

Consider Desma again. While she was working to get her consulting business off the ground, some friends called her up to ask whether she could help them by opening up a resale clothing shop.

Desma loved the idea. "I had talked about opening a resale shop one day and had started amassing stuff. My plan was that I would do it down the road, and my friends knew it," she says. But, "in conversation with them, they said they were getting a contract to start a job development program for women who were trying to move from welfare to work. They said, 'Desma, would you think about opening a resale shop now, because we have the space and the need for one?'" she says. These days, her resale clothing business brings in up to $30,000 per month.

Another of Desma's companies, a valet parking service, also started through her willingness to be open to her LifeNet and the opportunities it presents.

"I went to an event," Desma told me. "There was no valet parking available and someone said, 'If someone would just start this business, I swear they will never have to worry about having customers.'" Desma laughed. "I said, 'You can't joke about that around me, because I'm always looking for opportunities to employ people.'"

Desma did some research on what kinds of insurance and credentials she'd need for employees, and ended up launching Lady Valet. These days, though she's not actively looking for new contracts for the company, letting it survive on word-of-mouth as she focuses on her other businesses, Lady Valet still pulls in about $30,000 a year.

Who Do You Know? Just about Everyone

You've heard of six degrees of separation, right? That's the notion that everyone in the world is separated from everyone else by just six people. I know someone who knows someone who knows someone who knows you (that's just three degrees, but you get the idea). Another version of that theory is that if you make a list of 72 of the most important people who you know, you can reach anybody in the world.

Next time you're sitting in a restaurant, on a train, a bus, or an airplane, look at the person sitting next to you. You never know whether that person is somehow connected to someone in your LifeNet or someone you're trying to link to your LifeNet, or someone who *someday* you might need in your LifeNet. You just don't know who that person sitting next to you on the airplane knows. Even if your database of contacts is small right now, over time it will grow. Whether by six degrees of separation or the theory of 72, someone in your database will know the person you're trying to meet.

With the LifeNet approach, we build on the concept of interconnectedness behind these theories. That is, when you turn to the people, places, and resources around you, you put becoming a millionaire right in your Zone!

Here's how it looks (see Figure 3).

LifeNet Diagram

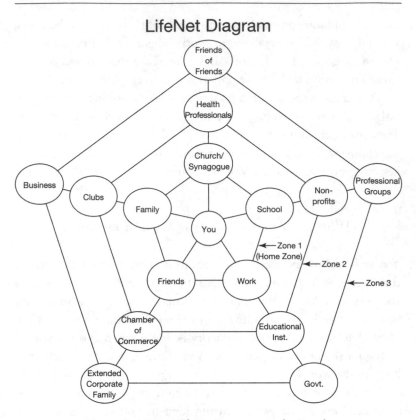

Figure 3. Your LifeNet Represents the People, Places, and Resources Familiar to You.

As you can see, you are in the middle. The spokes of your LifeNet radiate out, with each zone representing a new level of the LifeNet. There are three primary zones:

Zone 1 (Home Zone): The people, places, and resources closest to you. I also call this your Home Zone. These are people, places, and resources you know very well—the people you touch weekly and even daily. You're totally comfortable with this part of your LifeNet. These people are your life support system. You know you can go to them with any need and they'll respond in a heartbeat because they truly care about your well-being.

Zone 2: The people, places, and resources you know. The next zone is comprised of the people you know through the various clubs and social groups to which you and your family belong. They include places like your gym, a club or nonprofit organization you're actively involved with, even your doctor's office. This zone includes members of your health club, the people you see at your monthly chamber of commerce meetings, your chatty neighbor down the street, the other parents in your daughter's gymnastics class, your former college classmates—you get the idea.

Zone 3: The people, places, and resources you want to know. The final zone includes people you may have met previously but haven't spoken to in a while. They include the person your classmate introduced to you once, the one who has started a business similar to yours, the professional groups to which your friends belong, the nonprofit that is working to raise money for a cause you find worthy. This zone could also include resources at the city and state government level.

Now I want you to look at your LifeNet another way.

Notice in Figure 4, on the following page, that as you move from your Home Zone (Zone 1) to Zone 3, you move from operating locally, right in your own backyard, to operating globally. You've heard of the phrase, "Think globally, act locally"? That's how I want you to think of your LifeNet. Reaching out to all of the zones in your LifeNet will move you closer to the Millionaire Zone.

QUICK TIP: Are You Going It Alone? Five Signs

Are you going it alone and failing to use your LifeNet? Below are five signs you are holding yourself back from your full potential:

- You wonder why everyone else is making money and you're not.
- You're stressed about your job and wondering how to get ahead.
- You have money sitting in an account earning 5% or less—and it's not for emergencies.

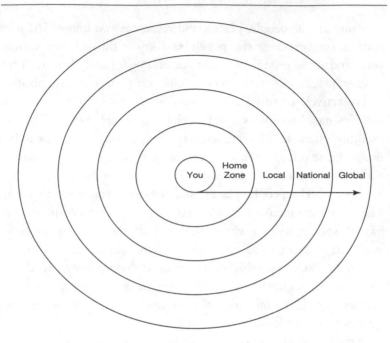

Figure 4. Your LifeNet—from Local to Global

- You've thought about working with a financial adviser or money coach but haven't.
- You have an idea that you've never tried to get off the ground.

Why You Can't Ignore Your LifeNet

Earlier we heard Edna Bell tell us how failing to connect with the people, places, and experiences around you will hold you back. By failing to turn to your LifeNet, you will miss out on money-making opportunities. You may hire or partner with someone you don't really know and trust. You may take a job (you discover afterward) that isn't really a great fit. You may go to a meeting not as prepared as you should have been.

Now, I'm not saying that your LifeNet always has the right answers or all the resources to get your venture off the ground. I *am* saying that by growing and harvesting your LifeNet, you greatly expand the possibilities for success.

Exercise: Take a few minutes to list ways that failing to use your LifeNet has held you back. Here are a few examples:

- You spend $150 to post a job-wanted ad, rather than going through the people in your LifeNet—for free!
- You spend days online trying to find a manufacturer for your product—with no certainty as to capabilities or reputation—rather than getting a qualified referral from your LifeNet.
- You don't do anything with your investments because you don't know what to do or whom to trust.
- You spend thousands of dollars to fly to job interviews or send out hundreds of resumes blindly when the chances of getting the job are remote because you have no contact, no one inside the hiring organization, rather than using your LifeNet to find insiders.

Now Wire Your LifeNet

Successful people use the elements familiar to them to get what they want. Your LifeNet wires together your contacts into a network of supporting people, places, and resources to help you reach your goals. But it's not enough to just carry around your LifeNet in your head. Particularly when you're just starting out, you need to spend time figuring out who the people you know are. What you will discover in the process, as I have, is that there are people and organizations you hadn't thought of in years—and those may be the very ones you can leverage to move into the Zone.

Remember what Desma said? It's worth repeating, because it shows how successful people operate. "I went through the list of family members, friends, and committees and other organizations

Your LifeNet

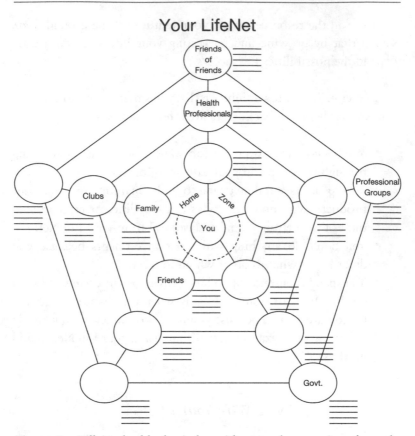

Figure 5. Fill in the blank circles with general categories of people, places, and resources you know. Then list specific people, places, and other resources that fall within those categories.

and sent out very personalized letters letting them know about our business, and then we would follow up from there."

Let's begin to wire your own LifeNet so we can identify the people, places, and resources at your fingertips. Take a look at your LifeNet in Figure 5.

Step 1: Take a close look at your LifeNet, starting with your Home Zone. Fill in the circles with friends, family and other key categories of people or places you interact with on a regular basis. Start by filling in a few. You've now built your Home Zone.

Step 2: Now build Zones 2 and 3. With a little thought, you'll be surprised how many circles at the end of the spokes on your LifeNet you can create. No matter how independent and isolated you think you are, you always have more supporting people and organizations than you realize.

Step 3: Identify your LifeNet members. For each circle in your LifeNet, list the actual names of people or organizations or resources that make up that category. I call these your LifeNet members. For instance, you might have "work" as a category. List the people or resources there who might be helpful to you. Examples are the head of a department you know or a peer right in your own group who's an expert Web designer. If you have government listed, think of those governmental entities you know: Is it City Hall? Is it the planning and zoning board for your town? If it's your health club, who do you know there? Other members? The manager? Trainers?

Now that you've wired your LifeNet, you're ready to start learning strategies for tapping into those people, places, and resources. But, first, let's look at ways you can make your LifeNet even bigger.

Grow Your LifeNet

How do you grow your LifeNet? It could be as easy as being open to the possibilities others suggest. I've mentioned talking to the people sitting near you when you travel or commute. I've added dozens of people to my LifeNet in just those ways.

Here's another example: My friend Diana wanted to get into real-estate investing but felt she didn't know enough to get started. One day she was at a conference on that topic. At a break, she headed over to the vending machine to buy herself a soda, but the machine ate her money. As she was kicking the machine, trying to get it to cough up her change, a fellow attendee approached her.

It turned out he regularly "flipped" houses—that is, bought houses and then fixed them up a bit and resold them for a nice profit. After their conversation, Diana decided to work for this investor to learn from him. She told me she would have worked for free just for the knowledge she could gain, but he's probably just as happy to have her on his team: She happens to be Puerto Rican and he wants her to help him break into the Hispanic market.

By wiring your LifeNet with as many circles and webs as possible, you begin to open your mind to a new way of thinking: that by making more connections and connecting the circles, you reach more people, grow your LifeNet, and, in doing so, greatly enhance your own chances of success.

It Really Does Work!

Talk to any business owner about how they got their business going, and you'll hear a story that involves their LifeNet. When Erica Zohar, our clothing guru featured in more detail in Chapter 6, started mulling over how to turn her passion for clothes into a clothing line, she mentioned her idea to friends.

One of those friends, a buddy from college back in Florida, told her: "Hey, my sister's a rep. You should talk to her."

So Erica called the sister, who worked as a buyer's representative for various clothing stores. Erica says now, "I was taught in 24 hours how the business works." She says she wouldn't move in a new direction now without first tapping into her network of friends and acquaintances.

"You'd be surprised how many people know someone who's in the field you're interested in, once you put the word out there," she says. "You can put out an e-mail: 'If anyone knows anyone in this industry, I'd love to meet them.'"

Tricia Ramer is another example. The former elementary school teacher now operates her business distributing cosmetics full-time. After just a year on the job working part-time, she was making $8,000 to $9,000 a month, well on her way to a seven-figure fortune.

What was her first step in starting her business?

"I made a list of every person I knew," Tricia says. "I thought,

Who would benefit from the products and who would benefit from the opportunity in the business?

"I call it planting seeds. Whether or not they're ready to jump on board with me, I'd plant a seed. And I'd water them," she says. "It was really just listening to people and listening to what was missing in their lives. Just planting a seed and talking to them at the pool or the store."

Tricia says she and her husband, who helps her with the business part-time, didn't focus solely on family and friends. "My husband sent letters to all the NFL football teams, to RV dealers to do welcome baskets. We marketed to hotels, casinos, Realtors, loan officers."

And expanding her LifeNet just came naturally. "You're out there running errands, meeting people, going to dinner with family, hanging out—it's part of your everyday life. It wasn't something I put on a calendar."

Remember Desma? This divorced mom of four kids is now in the Millionaire Zone, thanks in part to the way she focuses and relies on her LifeNet.

"No man is an island," she says. "You have to have people. And the best thing to do is to utilize the resources right at hand to advance what you're trying to do. And that's just to start. Then you expand out. It's like a circle you come back to. It really revolves back around that circle and then you expand again, and it continues to get bigger."

"You feed people and they get stronger," she continues. "It's sort of like with your family: Those stronger limbs come back to build and surround you with a stronger nest when you get old." No one describes how the LifeNet works better than Desma Reid-Coleman.

The End Zone

Here's what you learned in this chapter:

- Wire your LifeNet by filling in each of the three zones as I've outlined for you. In the process you'll probably realize that you know a lot more people, places, and resources than you thought you did!

- Ask your LifeNet for help. Share your thoughts and goals with the people who are eager to support you. Believe me, the people in your LifeNet want to support you—that's the power of your LifeNet. These are the people, places, and resources that are *most likely* to help you. They will offer support to you as you move from where you are now toward your goal of financial success.

- Give back. Remember this is not just about taking. It's a give-and-take process, where your LifeNet supports you and you support your LifeNet in any way you can.

- Talk to everyone in your LifeNet about what you're doing, but remember this is not just chatting. You need to persistently reach out to people, expressing your needs, asking questions, and offering, in turn, to help them.

- Be open to growing your LifeNet. Every time you meet someone, be open to the possibilities that person represents for you, your venture, and for the other people in your LifeNet. And always make a note of the names and contact information for the people you meet.

- Remember that weak ties are at least as important to growing your success as those people to whom you're really close.

In the next chapter, you'll learn how to make changes to get you from where you are now to where you want to be financially. You've heard me say it before: I'm not telling you to make changes in your life alone. Instead, you'll modify your current situation, taking small but significant steps to move toward the Millionaire Zone. Keep reading!

· 4 ·

Key 2: Redefine Your Comfort Zone

In Chapter 3, we saw how your LifeNet is the network of people, places, and resources around you, and how it can serve as a safety net as you work toward the Millionaire Zone. In this chapter, I want to focus on two words we've heard over and over in our lives in so many areas unrelated to money: Comfort Zone.

You see, in order to build a seven-figure fortune, you need to change the familiar patterns of your existence. *Why do I have to change?* you might be asking yourself.

You have to change because what you're doing right now is just not working. What is happening in your life right now—the way you operate daily—is not moving you toward the Millionaire Zone. That's why you bought this book, isn't it?

I know . . . how you live right now seems comfortable. That's why so many people stay in their Comfort Zone. Consider this: In my research of millionaires, 62% said they had to step outside of their Comfort Zone in order to be a financial success. But when I surveyed regular working Americans, 47% said they had not started their own business or attempted greater financial success because they were nervous about leaving their Comfort Zone.

These findings show you how important it is for you to start making some changes in your situation if you want to get ahead in life. But don't worry: I'll give you a clear and comfortable structure for doing just that. In this chapter, we'll answer the following questions: What are the things that define your Comfort Zone? Why is it so hard to change them? How do you change them? And what's the benefit of redefining your Comfort Zone? But first, here's Mark's story.

Mark's Story

Mark Fitzgerald started his career in corporate America, but it wasn't long before he realized he didn't like that he had to answer to someone else every working day.

"I really wanted to be able to control my own destiny rather than having someone else control it," Mark says now.

When he was just 30 years old, Mark and a coworker, Mike, had already been talking for a while about their unhappiness with their corporate jobs at a software company. "We worked closely together, and we shared a lot of thoughts about what we didn't like about the limited upside in corporate America on doing interesting things," Mark says. Plus, "the business we were in at the time was being acquired by a larger company and it was pretty chaotic on a day-to-day basis."

One day, after yet another meeting to discuss the company's merger, Mark started talking to Mike about their situation. "Mike, are you as tired of this as I am?" Mark asked.

"Yeah, this is showing me that I don't have any control over what's going to happen within the walls of corporate America," Mike said.

"We've talked a lot about doing something. What do you think?"

"I think we should talk seriously," Mike replied.

So on a gentleman's handshake, a partnership was begun, and Mike and Mark eventually ran a successful Internet consulting firm. "We spent lunch, nights, weekends for two months to meet and come up with a business plan of what we wanted to do and make sure we were financially prepared to not have an income for a while," Mark says.

"The first thing was to identify a market. It helped knowing who the potential clients were before we got started, because we already worked in that area. That definitely was part of the whole decision to head out on our own, knowing we had a niche market. We felt like we had a solid understanding of the marketplace, the IT world, and the development tools, so definitely we had a comfort level with that."

Mark and his buddy prepared in other ways before making the leap away from a steady paycheck. "The two of us had been saving aggressively and we were working with our wives to make sure they were on board, to make sure they were okay tapping into savings if there was no income coming in. We were prepared to go probably five to six months without any income, but fortunately we didn't have to do that. We had income our first month—not much but some," he says.

That was Mark's first venture, and since then he's started a series of successful companies. Right now he's running an online shoe store that pulls in $25 million dollars a year.

_____

Example from the Millionaire Zone
Bill Gates, founder, Microsoft
No. 1 on Forbes 400
Net worth: $51 billion
Key strategy: Redefine your Comfort Zone

Bill Gates would not be a household name if he were not adept at redefining his Comfort Zone. His success is essentially based on the fact that he didn't let comfortable thoughts define his actions.

He could have stayed and graduated from Harvard, instead of quitting to start his own computer company. He could have waited to see how the computer industry panned out. Instead, he and Paul Allen wrote that industry's history.

Aaron Boyd, author of *Smart Money: The Story of Bill Gates*, describes Gates as "one of the biggest gamblers in American business. Winning most of his bets has made him the wealthiest individual in America." In other words, Gates's success is based in large part on his ability to continually redefine his Comfort Zone—that is, reach out to new ideas, and place those bets.

Gates himself says that all he did was focus on building software, but you can tell he's always pushed ideas forward into new territory. "I've always rejected the term *entrepreneur* because it implies that you're an entrepreneur first and a software creator second. I didn't say, 'Oh, I'll start a company. What will it be? Cookies? Bread? Software?' No, I'm a software engineer and I decided to gather a team together. The team grew over time, built more and more software products, and did whatever was needed to drive that forward," he said, according to the 1997 *In the Company of Giants*.

Notice how he says "whatever was needed"? That's the thinking of someone unafraid of redefining his Comfort Zone.

CHAPTER CHECK-IN: *How Mark Redefined His Comfort Zone*

Mark was able to make big changes in his life, redefining his Comfort Zone, by:

* Partnering with a friend from work
* Moving into a venture similar to the job he was leaving
* Taking time to prepare before making the leap

How Mark Reached the Millionaire Zone
* Saved aggressively while still employed, allowing him to buy a triplex that he and his wife lived in; the tenants covered their

mortgage, allowing him to "roll anything I was making into the business without impacting us."

• Obtained his spouse's buy-in to tap savings for up to six months of living expenses in the event of no income.

• After minimal success with his first business, Mark did some consulting work for an old school friend who would become his partner in Grapevine, an online footwear company. His friend's contacts in the retail shoe business combined with Mark's own tech expertise allowed them to shift their Comfort Zones into an entirely new venture: online shoe sales.

• Created and expanded the company's presence on eBay to become the largest online footwear retailer in the world, in part by connecting with an eBay executive at a conference

• Because Grapevine was self-financed and had limited cash on hand, Mark decided to slow growth. He didn't want to risk taking on too much debt to feed the ever-increasing demand for his product. "If you're a small business, be sure to stay within your ability to keep up with your debt," says Mark.

Settle for Comfort or Make Millions?

Many people are just too afraid to step beyond the realm of what they know, even if what they know doesn't make them very happy. They settle for what's good enough. But there's no reason that what happened to Mark can't happen to you. The thing is, you can't do it without trying something new, something you're not doing right now. You need to change your Comfort Zone.

How did Mark do it? He did it by expanding and redefining his Comfort Zone. Sure, he left the very job that gave him a steady paycheck, the job that perfectly suited his skills. It might seem to you as though Mark left his Comfort Zone. But he didn't. Mark didn't just dive into something completely different. He took three important steps that, even as he reached out for something new, enabled him to stay close to his Comfort Zone, thus reducing the dangers of going out on his own.

What were those three steps? First, he partnered with his buddy Mike, someone he worked with and knew well. Second, they chose a venture that was closely tied to their current jobs in information technology, a field in which they were both well-versed. Third, they took some time to make plans and prepare for their new venture rather than quitting the safety of that steady paycheck cold turkey.

In other words, Mark expanded his Comfort Zone—that is, moved into a new venture—by relying heavily on, and staying close to, the very Comfort Zone that he knew so well.

No, the Paycheck Does Not Equal Comfort

Risking your own venture, as Mark did, doesn't mean you have to leave your job suddenly. Mark laid the groundwork first. Now read how Tricia Ramer did the same thing, redefining her Comfort Zone by first laying the groundwork.

For Tricia, the ability to leave her Comfort Zone only came after she had an "ah-ha!" moment about her steady paycheck. Tricia, a married mother of two, was a schoolteacher when she started selling cosmetics and products on the side. These days, she pulls in $8,000 to $9,000 a month working just part-time.

Back when she was first starting out, she juggled her teaching job and her Mary Kay sales—that was Tricia's method of laying the groundwork first. But soon her Mary Kay sales started taking off, to the point where she hired her mother as an assistant. (Remember wiring your LifeNet?!) Eventually, she started toying with the idea of quitting teaching. But that was a big leap to take.

"My biggest fear was not having the security of that monthly paycheck," she says.

Then a thought came to her. "One morning, I'm out running and a light bulb went on. I thought: *I'm not* guaranteed *a monthly paycheck. I have to show up every day for this.* That's when it dawned on me that Mary Kay is the same way. I just have to show up and do the work. I can't sit back and expect it to happen. I need to make it happen. And that's when I decided to make the jump."

What really happened in that "ah-ha!" moment? Tricia realized that her new venture was just another version of her familiar Comfort Zone. As long as she showed up every day and did her work, just as she was used to doing, her new venture would succeed.

Still, she didn't redefine her Comfort Zone after just one "ah-ha!" moment. Instead, she turned to her LifeNet for advice. She talked to her parents—they were both supportive. And she had many conversations with her husband, who is also a schoolteacher. "I looked at him and asked, 'How much is enough? When is enough enough?' He said, 'You're right. Quit teaching. Just do Mary Kay. And be a mom, set your own hours.' "

As Tricia's and Mark's stories show, you can redefine your Comfort Zone over time. There's no need to make huge drastic changes to your life all at once. But you do have to make some changes. Would Tricia or Mark ever be where they are today if they didn't change *something*? We all know the answer to that question.

Maybe you're someone who's not ready to make a jump—maybe you're in a job but, like Mark or Tricia, in the earlier stages and are just starting to think about it. Here are some signs that you may be ready for a life change:

- You're not happy in your current job.
- You wish you had more control over your destiny.
- You think there is no way to break out or get ahead.

Letting Go of the Security Blanket

In previous chapters, we explored the problems of going it alone. Now let's explore the problems of staying within your existing Comfort Zone. We need to find the right balance between being independent—that is, being willing to move in a new direction in our lives—yet relying on who and what we know to move safely in a new direction and thus achieve success. It's like letting go of the security blanket we had as children.

Why do you need to redefine your Comfort Zone to achieve financial success? Doing so is critical to changing your current life. And your life right now is not working—at least, it's not getting you to the Millionaire Zone.

The problem is, the longer you stay in your current Comfort Zone, the more likely it is you'll see change as a threat. Even those of us who regularly take risks in our lives often see an opportunity for change as a threat initially: "Wait! I like where I am. Why change?" But those who've become used to change remember that new opportunities bring excitement, a chance to grow and meet new people, and room for more financial success. Who do you know who became successful *without* making a change?

The sad result, then, is that inevitably we don't aim for something higher because we think it's not really attainable. We end up staying so long in one place that making any move at all just gets harder, until we let inertia take over our lives. The longer you're comfortable, the tougher it is to get off the couch and make something happen. So read on, to find out how to make some healthy changes.

What Is Your Comfort Zone?

I want to talk about how to redefine your Comfort Zone—as Mark, Tricia, and countless others have done—but to do that we first have to define it. This is easy: What makes you comfortable? What is it about your life's situation that makes you feel secure and familiar?

For most people, their Comfort Zone is made up of family, friends, our routine, our job, our home, our likes and dislikes. It's that place where everything feels easy and familiar, the place where you don't get overcome by feelings of anxiety. A steady paycheck is a big part of many people's Comfort Zone. The reason we stay in our Comfort Zone is because of the feeling of security we get from it.

Sometimes we even let our Comfort Zone define us, instead of the other way around. Even though we often feel trapped, we feel that there's no way to change our situation. The key is beginning to understand that the way your Comfort Zone has defined you may limit you and your family's opportunities and wealth.

Consider Carlos's story. It may sound familiar.

Letting Your Comfort Zone Define You

Carlos Torres is letting his Comfort Zone define him. He's a 56-year-old manager for a trucking company who's away from home far more than the average person. On top of that, the demands of the job put enormous pressure on him, at a time when he should be able to stop working and start enjoying life.

But Carlos faces steep medical costs. His and his wife's monthly insurance and prescriptions total more than $1,200 per month. More of us are likely to face this situation as time goes by, given that employers are shifting more health costs onto workers' shoulders.

But even if it's not the cost of health care, all of us can probably come up with two, three, or even six reasons why we can't change what we're doing—why we have to stay in our unfulfilling job rather than seek a promotion, why we can't risk losing that steady paycheck, why our dreams will never be met. The truth is, we don't have to let steep costs keep us locked into a boring, stressful, or un-fulfilling situation.

For years, Carlos has said he has no options but to stay on the job until he can retire. But he does have choices!

Carlos has an excellent reputation in his business and has worked for organizations that would very likely want to buy his services to train and educate other drivers. He has contacts with local government organizations. He also has a wife who wants to work. These are what form his LifeNet, waiting to be wired, but Carlos doesn't yet see that.

Carlos is really just hurting himself, preventing himself from moving forward by allowing his situation to define him.

But there are many different things he can do to make things better for himself. For instance, Carlos could begin working with his daughter, Theresa, in real-estate development, since she buys properties and could use him to remodel; a goal for Carlos would be to move into it full-time. Another option would be for him to go into business with his wife, funded in part by his daughter. A third idea: Carlos could go into business for himself doing any number of things from teaching to developing a new way for truckers to get safety training using the Internet.

Of course, many people stick to their Comfort Zone jobs because they think they can't afford to buy health insurance on the individual market. They hold on to those dead-end jobs because they know they have access to that employer-sponsored health care. Sound familiar?

Health-care insurance is obviously a big concern for Carlos; it's one of the reasons he's worked in such a tough job for so long.

The good news is there are some holes in that argument. The insurance you get through your employer is only getting more expensive, as companies fob off an increasing portion of rising health-care costs onto workers' shoulders. As health-care premiums have skyrocketed in recent years, workers paid a greater portion of those premiums: In 2005, employees paid 22.1% of health-care premiums, up from 14% in 1992, and that doesn't count other rising costs, such as higher deductibles and co-pays, that workers contend with, according to the Economic Policy Institute.

Compared to that, buying health insurance on the individual market may not be as expensive as you think. In fact, if you look at the total premium paid in employer group plans—that is, both what the employer and the employee pay—that premium is often much higher than an individual plan premium will cost, if you're in good health. That's because the group plan is riskier for the insurer because any worker, no matter how poor their health, can join the employer's plan. But when you buy insurance on the individual market, the insurance company assesses your health condition.

Check around to see what you'd pay on the individual market. Ask an independent insurance broker for help. One potential road-block: Because individual plans are underwritten—that is, your health is checked out—it might be tough for you to get a plan if you have a pre-existing medical condition and a gap of insurance cover-age of more than 60 days. But that doesn't mean you're out of luck. Read on for more ideas!

Here are some options:

- Look for a group plan through a professional organization. There are a wide variety of member associations offering group health insurance to their constituents. If you're not a member of a professional organization, it may be worth it to join for those benefits. Plus, you ramp up your LifeNet with additional contacts that way!
- Your spouse's health insurance. Often a spouse can start his or her own venture thanks to the health insurance the other spouse enjoys through an employer.
- Those with a history of bad health should check with their state's insurance department to see whether they qualify for a state-run plan—many states run plans for people who aren't eligible for commercial individual insurance.
- Don't forget COBRA. Federal laws require most employers to offer their employees access to COBRA for 18 months after they leave their job. It's a program that continues the com-pany's health insurance coverage for former employees, with premiums paid for by the former employees. The caution here is that COBRA only grants you access to the company's group policies, so you are required to pay the full premiums. Those COBRA premiums may be more than what you'd pay on the individual market.

• Health savings accounts (HSAs). There's a new tax-friendly vehicle aimed at encouraging people to save for their own health-care costs. You invest pre-tax money in a health savings account and all the money you take out of that account—including your untaxed contributions and any gains you earn on those savings—is tax-free as long as you spend the money on health-care costs. The catch is that if you have an HSA, you must buy a high-deductible health plan. Right now government rules call for a minimum deductible of $1,100 for individuals and $2,200 for families. Once you pay that amount (and note that with some plans it's higher than that), most HSA-eligible plans cover 100% of most medical expenses such as emergency room visits, hospitalization, lab tests, and prescriptions—all the things that would typically come with a health-insurance plan.

As I was writing this book, Theresa told me that Carlos finally got his workweek down to four days, leaving him with Fridays free. But a month after getting this good news the company told Carlos they needed him back. Poor Carlos. "I've got to stop working," he told his daughter. Theresa said she could see it on his face. At that moment, Theresa remembered an idea she'd been mulling for a while. As she walked around Carlos' home, looking at the impressive remodeling work he had done—from the kitchen, to the bathroom, to the floors, to the crown molding—she thought again: "What a shame not to use these skills to make money and get him out of this rut." So she broached the idea one last time: "Dad, you have amazing skills. I'm interested in converting apartments to condos if you have an interest in doing that with me." He perked up. For the first time in 10 years, he said: "I *am* interested." And today, he is actively purchasing his first building with his daughter.

Theresa will put in the money and he will oversee the project, getting a 50/50 share of profits. She will also provide a monthly stipend during the time he leaves his job and becomes eligible for Medicare as a supplement to his Social Security checks, so that he can cover his insurance costs. By having Carlos pay the insurance premiums, he can deduct them against the income he receives from Theresa. Because of his poor health, Carlos will look to join a group insurance program to get the best price.

Carlos will be able to stay within his Comfort Zone, albeit a new, expanded one that now involves his daughter putting up the money and his wife helping with the improvements and bookkeeping. He won't have to put up any of his money, but he will get to enjoy the rewards with a high chance of making more than he ever dreamed of—an estimated $200,000 for him alone on their first project, which will take about one year. I think Carlos now understands how he was letting his situation define his Comfort Zone and, in fact, doesn't need to leave the comfort of home at all.

Why We Don't Leave Our Comfort Zones

It's no wonder Carlos and many of us don't like to leave our Comfort Zones. Consider some fears that arise every time we lift a finger in the direction of moving outside our Comfort Zone. Do you face any of these fears?

- Fear of rejection
- Fear of embarrassing ourselves
- Fear of failure (afraid we "can't")
- Fear of change
- Fear of hurting others
- Fear of risk
- Fear of giving up a paycheck

Does the thought of taking that step into the unknown frighten you? We all know that fear. It pops up over and over again in everyone's life. It happens when we travel to a new place, buy our first home, start a new job, or just make a big purchase, like buying a car. Sometimes just meeting new people creates anxiety.

But you can't get to new places in your life without taking some risk. It's working through that nervousness and the risks that might arise—rethinking them, really—and getting to that new place that makes you grow into a stronger and more fulfilled person.

Haven't you been in a relationship or some other situation in which you knew you needed to make a change but were afraid to? Your relationship was going nowhere, but because you were afraid to leave, afraid to move outside your Comfort Zone, you stayed in it longer than you should have? Did you grow any more during that time? Chances are, no. Did you use that time to find the right person for your life? No. Did you feel better about yourself by staying in the relationship? Probably not. In fact, you probably didn't feel better until you actually did make a change, albeit after the initial shock. The same can be true when it comes to taking steps to make money.

Redefining Your Comfort Zone

We've talked about your Comfort Zone and how it can hold you back. Now let's redefine it by simply looking at it in a new way. Remember in the last chapter how I helped you wire your LifeNet? We looked at the people, places, and resources that make up your life's network. You probably noticed, as I did when I did the exercise for myself, that it's much, much larger than you ever thought.

Now take a look at the diagram in Figure 6.

Look familiar? Like the LifeNet diagram you completed on page 48? Look at your current Comfort Zone. That's the Comfort Zone you're familiar with—your current job, your current relationships, the people you know well and interact daily with. But notice,

Your Comfort Zone Today

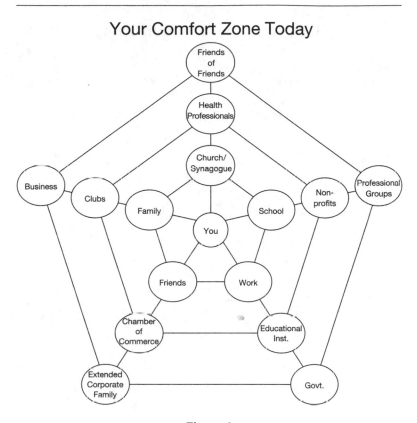

Figure 6.

in Figure 7, that as you expand your LifeNet, as we did in the last chapter, you also expand or redefine your Comfort Zone to be much broader than you thought.

By using your family, friends, and job, for instance, to connect with more people and places, you are in essence still operating within a framework of things that are familiar. You just might not know them directly or as well as those right around you on a regular basis.

So, rather than be afraid to step outside your Comfort Zone, you should recognize that you are actually still operating within it.

Growing Your Comfort Zone

Figure 7. Your Comfort Zone Expands as You Expand Your LifeNet.

It may sometimes *feel* new. Well, yes, it is new to some degree! But as you keep leveraging your LifeNet, it will get more comfortable. You will find yourself learning more, growing more. And most importantly, you will be opening yourself, your life, and your money to more opportunities.

I urge you to think a little outside the box: In what other small ways can you imagine your life changing and still keep that feeling of being secure and familiar?

Let's look at two people—a son and father—who both moved together to redefine their Comfort Zones and made money as a result.

QUICK TIP: Why You Should Redefine Your Comfort Zone

Re-think your Comfort Zone and you'll find it easier to make the changes you need in your life. That's because when you redefine your Comfort Zone, you will:

- Stay on familiar ground. Rather than feeling like you are leaving what is familiar when venturing out to try something new, you can instead feel like you are staying on well-known ground.
- Reduce fears. Redefining your Comfort Zone will allow you to reduce fears associated with making life changes. That's because you'll shore up support and get the knowledge you lack before moving forward. You're making changes, but you're staying to some extent within a familiar framework, so it's not as scary.
- Build strength in numbers. When you redefine your Comfort Zone, you also expand it to include more people and organizations. You'll enjoy strength in numbers as you venture out on your own by gaining valuable support from these new members.
- Improve yourself. The more you operate at the limits of your Comfort Zone, the more you will improve and enhance your own skills and knowledge, because you will be learning new things. At the same time, you will be constantly adding more members to your LifeNet.

David and His Dad: Two People in Different Comfort Zones

When David Randall was a young man just starting out in his career, he lived at home with his parents. He wanted desperately to be on his own, but didn't quite have the savings to buy his own home. At the same time, he also didn't like throwing money away by renting an apartment. He knew his father might lend him part of the money for the down payment, but he was afraid of asking, fearful of being rejected.

And he knew his father was very conservative with his money and was unlikely to want to throw it at something that might be the least bit risky. (This was back in the early 1980s, not long after the stagflation of the late 1970s, when prime rates had zoomed to more than 20%! So putting money into real estate wasn't perceived the way it is now.)

Two people trapped in their own Comfort Zones—David, afraid to ask his dad for help, and David's dad, unwilling to take risks with his money.

"My parents are very conservative financially. My father grew up in the Depression. The idea of putting a mortgage on his house [to loan David money] was anathema to him," David says.

But David figured out a neat trick for moving out of his Comfort Zone. He tapped another person in his LifeNet: his mother.

"The key thing was I enlisted my mother. Before I approached my dad, I told her what I wanted to do. I got her on my side. It's in her nature to help people."

David showed his mom some of the condos available in the area, and found one they both liked. David could afford it if his parents chipped in 50% of the down payment. David's mom then convinced her husband that the condo was a sound investment and that it could even be a place they could retire to one day.

"Besides," David told them, "I'm going to be earning more money soon and I'll easily be able to pay you back." His father agreed. When David moved a year later and sold the condo, real estate values had increased so much that he was able to hand his dad a check for $20,000. His father had tripled his money.

"When are we going to make our next investment?" his father asked when David handed him the check. Talk about redefining your Comfort Zone!

I love this story because it illustrates how two people operating outside their Comfort Zones can, by working together, move beyond their current Comfort Zones and ultimately make money. And you can also see how a member of David's LifeNet, his own mother, played a vital, supporting role. Without her, the deal may never have happened. And, perhaps more important, by stepping out and making a change, David's father could see how he could take risks within a safe zone and grow his wealth.

QUICK TIP: How to Get Someone Stuck in Their Comfort Zone to Invest

Just as David found it wasn't easy to get his father to invest with him, you may encounter someone resistant to change. His dad was stuck in his own Comfort Zone. Here's how to ease the fears of someone who's afraid to invest or otherwise partner with you:

- Make a financial case. Be able to succinctly explain the financial benefits of their participation. Lay out on paper your budget and expected returns.
- Enlist LifeNet support. Get support from a LifeNet member whom your potential partner knows and trusts. Make the case to them and get their input. See if that person will provide comfort in the form of additional insight to your potential partner.
- Prepare for the downside. Be able to explain the "what if" to your potential partner—what if the real estate market drops, for instance? Anticipate these what-ifs before engaging in a conversation.
- Put it in writing. Treat investment or other money-making opportunities as a business, even if (some experts would say, especially if) they are with friends or family. Put all the terms in writing. Include things such as how much money is being contributed, the purpose of the money, the goals for the venture, any expected return, and key dates. Then have both people sign the agreement. The more detailed your agreement, the fewer conflicts later.

One Person's Comfort Zone Is Another's
Risky Business

Sometimes, what feels like too much risk to one person won't daunt another person at all. You might see someone doing things that you could never do in a million years. That might make you perceive yourself as steady, safe, unlikely to take risks. But just because you're like that in some situations doesn't mean you're always like that. Your fear of certain things doesn't mean you'll never take a risk.

In fact, what feels risky to you may feel like smooth sailing to someone else, and vice versa. Take Susan Johnson. After her business was up and running, she was talking to an old family friend whom she hadn't seen in a while. She described how she had to buy a building that was big enough to hold the kitchen for her new business—delivering healthy, freshly cooked meals—and then buying a house five miles away, all in a city that was completely new and unknown to her and where she knew no one. (Her husband's job had been relocated to California, from Texas.)

Susan's friend responded, "Wow! Didn't the risk scare you? That was a big risk."

"I stopped dead when he said that," Susan says now. "I said, 'risk'? I never ever thought about it as a risk. I just didn't. Now that I'm smart enough to know, I think about it a lot more. Back then, we were just running on energy and passion."

For Susan, moving to a new place, starting her first business, in a field that she only knew through being a customer, did not feel risky. But that doesn't mean Susan never finds it difficult to leave her Comfort Zone. It's just that her Comfort Zone is different from her friend's.

Help from Surprising Places

When you're trying to redefine your Comfort Zone, it's a great idea to talk to the people in your LifeNet to get feedback. Some of them might have made a similar leap on their own, or maybe one of them always wished he'd done something like that and will encourage you to take the step they've yet to take.

But—and this is important!—don't expect the feedback you get to always be positive, and don't let any negative reaction stop you.

Tricia, when she was holding down her teaching job, parenting her two small children, and selling Mary Kay on the side, was nervous about quitting her full-time job. Before she quit, she talked to the various people in her life—with some surprising results.

"I had friends I consider good friends say 'You won't succeed,'" she says. "Then others say 'You've already succeeded. What are you afraid of?'"

But perhaps the most important conversation was with her boss, the principal at the school where she taught.

"I'm faced with a situation," she told him. "I can leave teaching, because I have some income from Mary Kay, but I have this fear of leaving."

The principal replied, "You have the opportunity. You have to do it. You have one chance to be a mom and this allows you to do that."

You won't always get positive feedback, but waiting for it can be well worth it.

Comfort Zone to Move Up within a Company

Some of you might think my idea of redefining your Comfort Zone is only for small, home-grown businesses or beginning entrepreneurs. Think again.

One of the top investment banks in the country, Goldman Sachs, uses the idea of a Comfort Zone to keep top performers, those with a lot of promise, on the edge of their seats and always learning. The company demands that some employees switch jobs every few years, so they keep learning, keep growing, and keep redefining their Comfort Zones.

"Up-and-comers cycle through jobs every few years, which keeps them at the edge of their comfort zones," said a Goldman Sachs manager, in a recent *Business Week* article. "They operate with their noses just above water, assuring top performance and a profound learning experience."

Goldman Sachs isn't the only firm to use that practice. But most companies I'm familiar with only use it in early training programs, when young people are just starting out. There are some great benefits to staying at the edge of your Comfort Zone, even if you're in a traditional job:

- Expand your LifeNet. As you move into a new venture, or to different parts of an organization, you'll meet more people and increase the number of members you can add to your LifeNet. Those people can serve as mentors, your next boss, or even a partner in your own venture.
- Develop more opportunities. Meeting more people and having more experiences means you'll be exposed to more opportunities. I've seen countless people who get a job offer in a different part of the organization because a manager has been able to see them in action, to assess their skills, and how they fit within an organization. Taking it a step further, many people—myself included—have developed an idea for their first venture after working inside a company and seeing firsthand the need for a new product or service.
- Negotiate a higher paycheck. For many people, the best way to move up is to move out. You'll often find it easier to get a better title and bigger paycheck by leaving your current job than by trying to improve your position from within. It's sad but it's a part of life. Only as you're walking out the door do employers wake up to the fact that they are losing a valued

contributor, and start to offer incentives to stay. But by that point, it's too late. If you're not ready to move out entirely, you may try to transfer out of your current group and into another within the same organization. Staying at the edge of your Comfort Zone and gaining new experiences will increase the odds of increasing your paycheck. And the more you move up in an organization, the better positioned you are to negotiate for higher compensation, bonus, and a total package.

If you're a manager in your own venture or within a company, chances are you'll have better results by keeping your employees at the edge of their Comfort Zone. Why? They'll be challenged and therefore less likely to leave. I can't tell you how many people I meet who tell me they want to leave their jobs because they're bored or not using their skills.

QUICK TIP: *Getting Better on the Job*

When you keep operating at the edge of your Comfort Zone, at work or elsewhere, you inevitably enhance your skills and knowledge—and your marketability both internally and externally. Here's how to do it:

- Company program. See if your company has a rotation program or if they'd consider allowing you to move from one group or division to another over a period of time, such as one to two years.
- Raise your hand. Offer to help on a program or project taking place in a group or division other than your own. You can also raise your hand to go overseas with your own company, where growth opportunities are often greater.
- Make it a win. Take on new tasks that you feel confident about tackling. You want to be able to point to a clear success, ideally one that improves the company or organization's bottom line.

The more successful you are, the more favorable others' opinions will be and the more opportunities that will come your way as a result.

The Power of Thinking Big

Remember we talked about Carlos Torres, the 56-year-old trucking manager? He refused to believe there were other ways for him to organize his finances, to live his life. Carlos really needed someone to help him see the bigger picture. Luckily, he listened when his LifeNet—in the form of his daughter Theresa—offered a valuable insight. Theresa's idea wasn't even so groundbreaking, just a simple suggestion based on Carlos's observable talents. But that idea of thinking big—thinking beyond your Comfort Zone—is a powerful one. Why? Because the only thing holding us back, really, is our own thought patterns. We let our current situation, our Comfort Zone, whatever it might be, define us. Instead, we have to expand our minds to think about the possible, rather than letting the impossible hold us back. We will then be as financially successful as we dare to be. It doesn't matter where you come from—working class, middle class, whatever—anyone and everyone has the power of thinking big.

I remember when I was just 12, riding my Schwinn bike home from school. I was thinking about the future and what I wanted to accomplish. Clearly, my mother's financial struggles had shaped me. So right then, riding down the middle of the street, I decided that I wanted to be financially successful. I wanted to do it by leading people, and I knew it would be up to me to make it happen. I saw myself helping people in need, those who were seeking help. And that's what I'm doing today!

Here's another example of thinking big: I used to work for a leading investment firm that helped big pension funds manage their money. The firm had a stock index similar to the S&P 500, except it represented truly all the companies in the stock market. It had some unique value if you wanted to know how the entire market was performing. I said to myself, "Okay, Jen, if you want to make this index a household name in the investment world, what do you have to do?" I came up with two answers: 1) Make it available in real time, and 2) Try to get the number-one financial news network to use it regularly. It was a long shot, but I accomplished both goals, and to this day the CEO of the company can turn on the television and see his index featured. That's about $2 million worth of free advertising every year. Of course, that CEO remembers me to this day.

When I was getting my first company off the ground, I never thought *I can't call that person—he's too rich* . . . or famous, or well-connected or powerful. No! I just picked up the phone. What I found is that people like the founder of Mrs. Fields Cookies, the former chief technology officer of E*Trade, executives of Fortune 500 companies, and many others believed in my concept and offered their support. How did I do it? Of course I had to believe in my message and so did they. But it came down to thinking big, and not being afraid to ask. And once I did ask and found some success, I expanded my Comfort Zone and became more confident as a result. And you can, too, if you think big!

QUICK TIP: How to Connect with the Top

Many people are afraid of connecting with people at the top because they're intimidated. Here are a few examples of people who took a deep breath and made it happen.

- Andrew: Andrew saw the CEO of a major financial institution speak at a conference. The 24-year-old was starting to make money as a stockbroker but realized that if he didn't move into something bigger and better, chances are he never would. So he sent a letter to the CEO, asking if he'd finance

Andrew's way through graduate school since he didn't have the money. Within days, Andrew got a call from one of the CEO's top lieutenants who said, "We can't write you a check but we can give you a job and pay part of your tuition." Andrew took that job, and since then has worked for several nationally known CEOs, putting himself in a position to start his own venture with other people's money.

- Kit: Kit recently attended a conference where the CEO of a major media company spoke on a panel. Not surprisingly, afterward the CEO was surrounded by a swarm of people. Kit sat on the sidelines and waited for the people to clear out. He then approached the CEO's assistant and asked if he could have a brief word with him. Kit ended up having 10 quiet minutes walking the CEO into and up an elevator and got just what he wanted: an introduction and meeting with a senior executive at the company.

- Me: I remember meeting the CEO of a leading Internet company when I was first starting out. I had talked to one of his senior executives about helping them build their business as I was building mine. I had given him a business plan, as requested, and lo and behold I got the meeting. I walked into a conference room where he had a team of people. Boy, was I nervous! I told myself to set aside my fears, focus on the moment, and act like an equal. The more you see yourself as an equal, the more confidently you will communicate and the more open to your message the recipient will be. The CEO later told me he decided right then and there we would work together.

Putting It into Action

Right now, I'd like you to think about the fears that arise when you think about leaving your Comfort Zone to make more money. Write them down here.

When I think about taking steps to change my financial situation, I'm afraid that:

_____

_____

_____

_____

_____

_____

You've read how real people have redefined their Comfort Zones and made positive changes. I want you to do the same. After each fear, I want you to ask yourself: "How can I use my LifeNet to overcome the fear?" An example is Mark Fitzgerald using his friend Mike and the knowledge they both had in information technology to overcome the fear of failure. Another example is Carlos Torres working with his daughter to overcome the fear of risk and financial loss. And yet another is Tricia, who stayed in her current job as a teacher and used her family and friends to help her build her business.

So step back, look at the list of fears you just wrote, and find the members of your LifeNet who can bring comfort to those fears in some tangible way.

Fears   *LifeNet Solutions*

_____   _____

_____   _____

_____   _____

_____   _____

_____   _____

The End Zone

Think about the stories of real people in this chapter. These people didn't dive into completely alien territory. They only shifted their Comfort Zones slightly. Let's sum up how to do this:

- Define your current Comfort Zone. What is familiar to you? What is safe? Stop and think about the specific structure in which you operate, including your current job, your current home, and your immediate friends.
- Envision your LifeNet. Step back, and review the people, places and experiences you know or have some relationship with, even if not direct. Chances are, there are many, many more than you realize. And each of those is already familiar to you. Envision the members of your LifeNet as part of your Comfort Zone.
- Your LifeNet becomes your Comfort Zone. Now that you've recognized that many people and entities make up your LifeNet, you can view your Comfort Zone in the same way. Your Comfort Zone now encompasses your LifeNet and is larger than you originally thought. Your Comfort Zone will always expand as you increase members of your LifeNet.
- Redefining your Comfort Zone means taking small steps toward your goals. All the while, elements of your Comfort Zone are backing you up, putting success within your grasp.
- You'll find help in surprising places, so don't be afraid to talk to people about what you're hoping to do. Being willing to share your ideas and goals for the future is absolutely essential to moving forward.
- Talk to important people in key positions. Carry yourself as an equal, and you'll be amazed what doors will open for you.
- Don't compare. Each of us has different LifeNets and Comfort Zones. Don't think that another person's Comfort Zone should be yours.

- Re-think the security of that guaranteed monthly paycheck. Your hard work can guarantee any paycheck.
- Don't abandon your Comfort Zone, and don't get stuck in it. Redefine it! Don't let your Comfort Zone define you. Take control over it and put it to work for you.

When you have the confidence to redefine your Comfort Zone:

- The number of possibilities and opportunities expands exponentially.
- You stay in familiar territory, so the fear of rejection doesn't hold you back.
- "Can't" becomes "can."
- You feel more in control.
- Your confidence will increase.
- Your chances for success will increase.

Below is a quiz, which will assess where you fall in the "risk continuum"—that is, how entrenched are you in your own Comfort Zone? After you take the quiz, I offer an analysis of the results and offer guidance based on your risk personality as you prepare to reach the Millionaire Zone.

Remember, having envisioned some minor changes to your life that do not involve moving outside your Comfort Zone, you can begin to realize the first secret to overcoming your fears and making real changes in your life.

Your Zone can stretch to accommodate the changes you want, without giving up the *Comfort*! By staying within yourself, you begin to recognize that any change you can imagine can happen. All you need to do is redefine your Comfort Zone. It's all up to you!

TAKE THE QUIZ: Where's Your Comfort Zone?

This exercise will help define the importance of your Comfort Zone. You may be too reliant on your Comfort Zone and hesitant to make the changes that will affect your financial future. Or you may be too independent for your own good. Answer the following questions to find out where you stand. Pick the one that's closest to your personality.

1. When it comes to keeping in touch with family:
   a) You have their numbers on speed dial and talk almost every day.
   b) You plan a get-together about once a month.
   c) You're lucky if you see them on big holidays.

2. You remember your friends' birthdays:
   a) Always
   b) Sometimes
   c) Rarely

3. When it comes to planning out your future, you:
   a) Know exactly where you will be five years from now
   b) Have a vague idea of what you'd like to be doing in the future
   c) Just worry about making it through the week

4. The last time you bought a car, you:
   a) Test-drove all comparable models and explored all the financing options
   b) Knew what you wanted and had an idea for how you'd pay for it
   c) Went with a friend to help pick out a car and ended up driving away with one of your own

5. When it comes to finances, you:
   a) Know your exact balance in each account all the time
   b) Have a pretty good idea of what you have, but don't obsess about it

   c) Always have to look it up and are often surprised by the numbers

6. You have plans on Friday night at 8 p.m. to go to the movies with a friend. Another friend calls at 6 p.m. with an extra concert ticket. It's a band you've always wanted to see. You:
   a) Stick with your existing plans. You don't think your friend would have minded, but you hate changing your plans at such late notice
   b) Agree to go to the concert, but only if you can find another ticket for your friend.
   c) Go to the concert. You feel bad, but you know your friend will understand. You do stuff like this all the time.

7. Which of the following best describes how well you know yourself?
   a) I know all of my likes and dislikes and don't like to stray from them.
   b) I know myself pretty well but am sometimes surprised by how I react to a situation.
   c) I think I know myself well, but my friends and family would describe me differently.

8. How much sleep do you get every night?
   a) 7.25 hours
   b) About 6 or 7
   c) It's different every night.

9. Your friend has invited you for a weekend getaway, but you have a huge deadline on Monday. You:
   a) Pass on the trip so you can stay home and get your work done
   b) Go, but come home early so you can get your work done on Sunday

c) Go but without a plan for doing your work. You'll get it done somehow.

10. You would like to be described as:
a) Diligent
b) Level-headed
c) Creative

11. When you're driving somewhere you've only been once before, you:
a) Pull out the map and get exact directions
b) Glance at a map but wing it from there
c) Rely on your gut. You can always ask for directions if you get lost.

Results

If you answered mostly "a":

Your Comfort Zone is extremely important to you. You find comfort and security in planning your future and knowing exactly what you want. You know your likes and dislikes very well. You're likely terrified by the idea of starting a new job or leaving your existing one for a new opportunity. And you wouldn't think of making a new purchase or starting a new venture without exploring every option available. When it comes to making your millions, you've got knowledge and planning on your side. That will serve you well. When examining your Comfort Zone, look to partner with someone who is more spontaneous and who will urge you to move forward when you feel the urge to do more research.

If you answered mostly "b":

Your Comfort Zone is important to you, but you're not afraid of going it alone. You take a balanced approach to life. You'll plan and research when necessary but also see the value of being spontaneous when the situation calls for it. You know your likes and dislikes, but you are usually willing to try something new. You are excited by the prospect of a new opportunity and will go into it willingly, but not without making sure you've covered your bases. When it comes to making your millions, you will do well. Just be sure you know exactly when to plan and when to be spontaneous. Stay within your Comfort Zone when it suits you, but don't be afraid to look beyond it.

If you answered mostly "c":

Your Comfort Zone isn't all that important to you. You're independent and like to do things your own way. You often go against the grain. You're creative and spontaneous. You don't like to plan out your life. You're probably not all that good at it anyway. You tend not to look before you leap. You love the thrill of your life but have also made some whopping mistakes. Take heart, when it comes to making your millions, your instincts will serve you well. When examining your Comfort Zone, look to partner with someone whose strength is research and planning. Find someone who will slow you down when all you want to do is move ahead.

· 5 ·

Key 3: Ready, Set . . . Home Zone

We all know the saying "Home is where the heart is." The world has become a cynical place, but we can still recognize that that expression is rooted in a truth: that our home and all of the people and places we know well are central to our well-being.

This chapter is all about how your most familiar environment—your home, your core experiences, your family, your workplace, all the people and places you know well—play a fundamental role in how you move your financial life up to a new level. These familiar things are some of your richest sources of ideas and support for your new venture.

We talked in the last chapter about how important it is to redefine your Comfort Zone, to try things you've never tried before if you want to un-stick your life and move toward a new place.

Now I'm going to suggest something that may sound contradictory. As we discussed in the last chapter, you've got to leave your comfortable spot on the couch to reach the Millionaire Zone. Yet the best way to succeed when you step into the unfamiliar ground of your new venture is to focus on the areas in your life that you know best. As I said in Chapter 2, I call these areas your Home Zone.

CHAPTER CHECK-IN: Why Start with Your Home Zone?

- Your most familiar place: Your Home Zone is made up of the people, places, and resources you know best, those with which you're most comfortable.
- Rich with ideas and support: Your Home Zone can give you ideas to make money, the resources to do it, and the people to give you great advice and support.
- Concern for your success: Your Home Zone is where most of the people who care about you reside. These are people who will take the greatest interest in your well-being and financial success and help you execute your goals, as long as you share them.

Let me give you an example of someone who used his Home Zone to create a booming business for himself and his family.

Wayne's Story

Wayne Finkel is an auditor. He spent years working at a midsize auditing firm keeping an eye on the books kept by some of the largest companies in this country. Wayne roots out fraud and corruption—the kind that took down Enron and WorldCom—and assures his customers (and their shareholders) that their financial policies and practices are sound.

Wayne had a good job, but he knew he could do a much better job than some of the independent contractors his company hired when it had more work than it could handle.

So he talked to a coworker about becoming partners and setting up their own auditing firm. And he talked to others at the company as well. One man who worked under him at the firm said, "Wayne, any work I have, I'll throw your way."

Some of the 40-plus independent contractors he had worked with also kept him in mind as they moved from firm to firm.

"Wayne," they'd call up and say, "I hear you're contracting. Have you got anybody available next week? We've got some business for you."

Then Wayne set up a time frame for launching out on his own.

"I gave 60 days' notice," he told me. "So I'm working for one company and on the side starting my own business."

He and his partner each put in $5,000. "I only needed to pay myself for a couple of weeks to get by until I built up some receivables," Wayne says.

Then Wayne turned to another part of his Home Zone—his wife, Charlene Rios—to build their wealth further. Not only does Charlene handle the company's books but she's taken what the company earns and invested it in real estate. Thanks to Charlene, they now own two properties, one of which houses their business. They bought one commercial building in an up-and-coming area for $220,000. In just three years, its value jumped to $700,000. Not only did they take a giant leap closer to a seven-figure fortune Zone by leveraging their $44,000 down payment into a $480,000 gain, they stopped paying rent to someone else.

Finally, they did what many others fail to do: They sought advice when they faced situations they didn't understand. "Wayne always likes to cover his bases," says Charlene.

Again, their Home Zone played a key part. Through a friend of a friend they met an attorney who showed them an important strategy for protecting their assets. Rather than purchasing the real estate in their own names, as most people would have done, they set up a limited liability company (LLC) and had the LLC purchase the properties.

The benefit? If they were to get sued for any reason—whether through Wayne's business or by the tenants renting their properties—their personal assets remain protected. This is a great example of realizing that you can't always be an expert in everything. By starting with your Home Zone, you can both make real money and protect what you have.

With Charlene's help, Wayne's business, Unified Examiners, throws off $2 million a year in revenue, and at the same time they've grown their personal net worth through their real estate company, Unified Examiners LLC.

CHAPTER CHECK-IN: *How Wayne Started with His Home Zone*

- Identified a need for auditing services through his daily job, thereby allowing him to stick with what he knows best
- Decided to learn as much as he could from his boss to improve his knowledge and skills before starting his own business
- Tapped wife, Charlene, to manage the company books, serve as a sounding board to Wayne, and buy and renovate buildings
- Partnered with a coworker from his job to launch his new venture
- Turned colleagues into sources of new customers by always treating them with respect
- Gave two months' notice instead of the standard two weeks' to build goodwill

---

Example from the Millionaire Zone
Mary Kay Ash, founder, Mary Kay Cosmetics
Net Worth: Unknown
Key Strategy: Ready, Set . . . Home Zone

The late Mary Kay Ash came up with the idea for her cosmetics company—which grew to become the largest direct seller of skin care and cosmetics in the United States—sitting at her kitchen table, mulling over the things she liked and didn't like about her 25-year career in direct sales.

That is, she took a look at what she knew—her work experience, part of her Home Zone—and made a list of its advantages and disadvantages. When she realized that she had the makings of a great idea for a new company, she took her life savings of $5,000, tapped another part of her Home Zone for help—her 20-year-old son—and opened her first store in Dallas in 1963. She started out with just nine independent beauty consultants. Mary Kay Ash also based the company's philosophy strongly on her Christian faith, telling her people to focus on God first, family second, and work third. Based on these principles, she encouraged women and gave them new opportunities for their own personal and financial success. Of course, the very basis of the company's strategy is to encourage its beauty consultants—who now number in the hundreds of thousands—to turn to their LifeNets to generate new business.

The Secret: Tap Your Home Zone

Wayne Finkel makes success sound easy, right? The only reason it sounds easy is because he worked with his Home Zone long before quitting his day job, and he tapped his Home Zone even after he quit his job and started working full-time on his own independent practice. How exactly did he do this?

First, the very nature of his new company is founded on what he knows best: auditing. He saw a need for services like his, so he decided to stretch out into his own business. Using your talents—the *experiences* that are familiar to you—is one example of using your Home Zone.

Second, before he left his full-time salaried job, he created demand for his services by talking to coworkers and potential clients he knew who could help him. "I had been chatting with people for a year before," he says. That means he looked around at familiar things—the people and companies he worked with at his job—and leveraged that knowledge to pave the way for his future success.

How Wayne and Charlene Reached the Millionaire Zone
- Understood the gap in the market for his services and the value he could provide
- Began his business with just $5,000 in personal funds, a partner, and a plan
- Purchased a commercial building in an area they were familiar with to stop paying rent to someone else and further built their own wealth
- Established a company to own their real estate, thereby reducing any personal losses in the event of a lawsuit

Your Workplace . . . and Other Home Zones

The bedrock of Wayne's new venture was based on his job, obviously a key part of his Home Zone. He saw the potential for his own successful business, because the people and companies with whom he worked as an employee needed timely and dependable auditing. He worked at a company that needed the very services he could provide.

Where you work is one component of your Home Zone. You know people there, you see needs that must be met, you see where demand is. Work is a prime place to consider when you look around your world for ideas on what type of venture might be successful. And, of course, if you're looking to push your salary higher by moving up within your company, you need to focus on the people in the firm who can help you do that, or consider how your skills might translate into higher income at another company. Once you know what idea you want to pursue, your Home Zone again becomes useful as a source of potential employees, customers, support, and other resources, including a source of people who might hire you.

Dr. Pooper Scooper is another instance of using your work experience as a means to greater income. Richard Roy was running his own business as a landscape gardener in New Jersey, and one thing kept getting in his way.

"Every lawn with dogs . . . well, I was stepping in the stuff," Richard says with a laugh. "I was joking for several years that I was going to do 'Doodie-Free.' "

Then after reading about a couple of people in other states that made a good living at cleaning dog messes off people's lawns, Richard met with a small-business adviser.

"I'd hire you immediately for the stuff on my own lawn," the adviser said. Thus was Dr. Pooper Scooper born. In three years, Richard has gone from earning just $800 a week managing someone's properties and doing a bit of landscaping on the side to a full-time landscaping business generating about $1,000 a week and now to a business that is growing by leaps and bounds, creating $3,000 a week. He's tripled the number of customers since last year and has hired his first full-time employee. Richard spotted an opportunity right in front of him and used it to move him closer to the Zone.

I've tapped my own family to help me build my wealth, and what a difference it's made! After I sold my first company, I put some of the money I made into real-estate properties, and asked my mother to manage them for me. She already had experience buying and selling duplexes. With her help, I turned $200,000 into $1 million in four years. Mom plays an essential, vital role in my Home Zone. Besides managing the properties, she identifies prospective real estate and screens tenants. My brother helps out, bringing his handyman skills whenever something needs fixing. Just as Desma's mother, who manages Desma's resale store for her, plays a strong supporting role in Desma's career, my parents and other family members have been critical to my success. Their help has enabled me to stay focused on other parts of my business and take me further into the Zone in just three years.

This Is Your Home Zone

So you can see there are a variety of people, places, and experiences that make up your Home Zone. Essentially it's where you operate on a daily or at least regular basis. There are five primary elements to your Home Zone, though the exact number may change depending on how you live your life.

Family. This means your spouse, your kids, and anyone else in your own home, plus your relatives—parents, siblings, cousins—whether they live nearby or across the country. The beauty of the Internet means your Home Zone is not limited geographically anymore.

Friends. Friends' houses, restaurants, any local clubs you belong to. That is, any social locales. Your Home Zone includes your experiences at these places, but also the people. Maybe your next-door neighbor knows all about jewelry-making, a hobby you love that you'd like to turn into a side business. Ask her!

Spiritual Center. Any place of worship or spiritual contemplation where you gather or meet with like-minded people on a regular basis.

School. This could be any classes you take—that is, the people you meet there, the ideas you find there—as well as your college alumni association, your high school reunions, or the people you know through your kids' schools.

Work. Just like Wayne, Dr. Pooper Scooper, and others, you may have a wealth of ideas and resources sitting right in front of you every day when you go to work. Think about it, write it down, tap into it.

QUICK TIP: How Your Home Zone Helps You

The people, places, and resources within your Home Zone can provide a myriad of benefits, such as:

- Ideas
- Information
- Introductions
- Practical support
- Financial support
- Emotional support

Your Home Zone

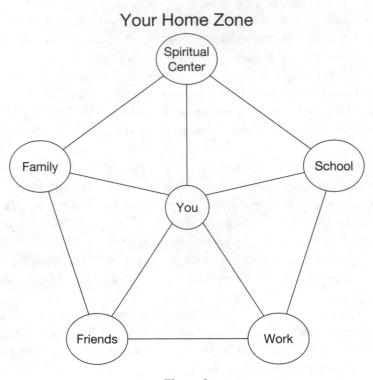

Figure 8.

People, But Also Much More

Now, what do you immediately think of when you think of the five elements in these circles? Probably people! People are a key, but each of these centers is a source for more than just the people you know there. They are a source for the following.

Ideas. The way life is, someone or something might just give you the spark of an idea to help your business take off or take it to the next level, just as with Dr. Pooper Scooper.

I remember when I worked for a large bank. The bank began offering a family-oriented credit card. The problem was that thousands of families who wanted the card had poor credit or no established credit, so they were being turned down. It dawned on me that these people needed help building their credit; after all, you need good credit to buy a home or build a business or pretty much do anything today. After investigating further, I discovered that the bank had no available program to help consumers in that area, so I decided to build an easy credit improvement kit, which I now call the Quick & Easy Credit Kit (www.easycreditkit.com). My boss, the head of the credit group said, "We could help these people by offering this kit and helping them improve their credit." Thus, my Home Zone—my on-the-job experience—was the source of an idea. I could see directly how not just one but thousands of people had a real need for this.

Information. Information can help you grow your wealth even if you're in a job right now, working for someone else. Listen to Andy Henson's story. Andy recently made a job change from corporate America to a more entrepreneurial partnership. Looking back, he feels he avoided what could have been a disastrous decision. He was on the verge of accepting a job overseas with a well-known company—a job considered the crème de la crème in his profession—until he called a friend at the company.

"I've been offered a really exciting position in Asia with your company," he said. "What can you tell me about the business there?" The friend was truthful: "It's in a bit of a shambles. Lots of people have left."

Wow, Andy thought. *I need to ask more questions to understand what I'm getting into.* The friend went a step further: He told him what salary he thought others in similar roles were making, helping Andy in his negotiations. Andy took that information and asked for more money—pointing to what others were making—and got it. In fact, his final offer was a full 20% higher than the original compensation package. He also reached out to others in his Home Zone, another close friend and adviser named Rich. Andy had known Rich a long time, and Rich, coincidentally, knew the founder of the start-up partnership company Andy was also considering.

"Originally I was thinking it would be best for you to take that overseas job," Rich said to Andy. "But there are some risks there.

The economy could falter and then what? You'd be out of work and in Asia. And I can tell you about the people at this other partnership. It's a start-up, but these guys have reputable financial backers. For you to be able to get into that firm as one of the top four owners and possibly make some *real* money . . . well, you'll never get this kind of opportunity again."

Andy absorbed all this information, asked tougher questions about the Asia job, and ultimately decided to say good-bye to corporate life in favor of the entrepreneurial route. But all the information and negotiations he did with the corporation weren't for naught: Andy was able to use that information to negotiate a better package, again about 20% more than the original offer, plus more ownership in the entrepreneurial venture. He has now positioned himself to be well into the Millionaire Zone upon the planned sale of the firm, at an estimated $5–10 million for him alone.

QUICK TIP: *Moving Up the Corporate Ladder*

Your LifeNet can provide valuable information and resources if your aim is to move up the corporate ladder, whether at your current company or to a new company. Tap your LifeNet for the following information:

- Assess your worth: Talk to coworkers at your company or the company you're considering to find out what they think you should be paid. Also, try friends and contacts at the company's competitors. They're in a better position than you to know what your peers are earning.
- Get advice: Talk to peers and advisers outside the company who can give you insight and perspective. You might find that they know something about the company or the industry— even your prospective boss!—that you don't know.
- Compile competing offers: The more offers you have, the better positioned you are to make more money. Use your LifeNet to find out about other opportunities and get in front of more

prospective employers. Don't be afraid to tell them of an offer already on the table; it makes you look in demand.

• Negotiate: Use the information about what you're worth and the offers already in hand to negotiate compensation, title, and even ownership. Let the facts speak for themselves. Remember, the more information you have gathered from your LifeNet and the more facts you can present, the better your chance of getting paid substantially more than you were before—and the better positioned you are for your next move.

Introductions. Members of your LifeNet can provide crucial contacts, whether for new customers or even financing to get a venture going, as Marnie Walker found out when she tried to get financing for her transportation business while still working full-time at another job. "I had a friend whose husband was president of a venture capital firm," she says. "I also went to colleagues I knew who had positions in banks. I said, 'This is what I want to do. What do I have to do to get the money and what do I do to make it easy for someone like you to give me the money?' Then, I asked for a contact in the bank so that I wasn't going to someone cold; I went to three or four banks and I got the money. It was huge to be able to get access and get to the right people. A referral is the best endorsement." Marnie eventually sold her business for $10 million.

Practical Support. This type of support can come in many forms, from teaching, where someone in your Home Zone helps you fill in your knowledge and skill gaps, to talent and resources. Perhaps you can ask a friend who's started her own business to review your business plan, or to check out an advertising proposal aimed at promoting your business tools or equipment to help you reach the Zone.

Resources can be anything from free or low-cost office space to a graphic designer offering to create your logo in exchange for an ad on your Web site.

Financial Support. Look to the people in your Home Zone and think about whether *they* could benefit by lending you financial support. That is, don't just look at them financing *your* success. Instead, see how an investment in your business can earn them a legitimate financial return.

Remember David Randall and his parents, from Chapter 4? He wanted to buy his first home, but he knew his father, having grown up during the Depression, would be hesitant to take on more debt. David enlisted his mother to help convince his dad that this would be a sound investment. Their combined effort worked, and 10 months later David sold the condo and handed his father a check for *triple the amount David had borrowed.*

"I'll never forget the expression on his face," David says. "I knew how much it meant to him that he had trusted me on this and I had not only come through, but he also had made money. I handed him the check and he said, 'David, when is our next investment?' I can't tell you what that felt like. That was magic to me."

But family members are not the only potential source of this kind of support. Many people venturing out on their own for the first time seek support from friends and family. In fact, in the formal venture capital world, often your "friends and family round of financing" will be your first as you start to grow your business. Friends and family can provide funding and, in exchange, get ownership in the company or they can provide a loan that is repaid at an agreed-upon interest rate. Listen to David's advice: "When you involve your family, your friends, someone believes in you and you take a chance. If you really know what you're doing and you're confident, everybody can win. I won because I got a foothold in real-estate ownership. I won because the return I made on the investment allowed me to then put money in the next house. And my dad won because he helped his son and made money."

Banks and outside investors are another possible source of funding. With a well-developed business plan that clearly delineates who your customers will be, why they'll choose your product or service, and how your idea will generate money, a bank loan agent or an investor is much likelier to consider funding you. Of course, your Home Zone can help here, too: Get a referral to a bank officer or venture capitalist from someone in your Home Zone.

QUICK TIP: How to Raise Money from Friends and Family

One of the most common ways of financing a new venture—like turning an idea into profits—is to raise money from people you know best: friends and family members. Here's how to do it:

- Create a plan. You'll need to make a case for the venture, including a financial case. A PowerPoint presentation will work well, although you can create a full business plan using any of the many templates available. Be sure it covers these key areas: the need, the opportunity, the product/service you plan to provide to address the need, plans for marketing, expected costs and revenues, and key goals with deadlines.
- Involve them. Consider involving friends or family from your LifeNet who can provide some assistance to you and your venture, perhaps expertise or knowledge about the industry. Also, look for someone who might have financial resources—money to invest—as well as an interest in your project.
- Loan or ownership. Once you've determined your financial needs, you'll need to decide if you want to ask for a loan at a fixed interest rate over a fixed period of time or offer direct ownership in your venture. Remember, the more investors, the more people you need to keep happy, so fewer is sometimes better.
- Document it. Be sure to develop a formal written agreement. Consider finding an attorney through your LifeNet who can assist in drafting your document or reviewing it at a reduced cost.
- Keep them posted. Your friends and family will be your first investors. Just as if they were investing in a mutual fund that provides quarterly performance reports, you need to update them regularly on your progress.

Emotional Support. The people in your Home Zone can also offer various forms of emotional support. This type of support is harder to quantify but just as necessary when you're working to get your venture off the ground.

Seek out the people in your Home Zone who will be your cheerleaders, who will keep you going during the tougher times. Don't wait until you need them to reach out. Do it now so they feel part of the process. As pilots say, "Have 'em with you at takeoff if you want 'em there on the landing!"

The Wrong (and Right) Way

To get a sense of why sticking with your Home Zone is such a good idea, consider what happens when we *don't* use familiar territory. I once had the opportunity to compare how my friends Sarah Banks and Kevin DiCerbo—they don't know each other—went about hiring an employee. Sarah decided to go online to a job listing board with no screening criteria. She did it because it was fast and cheap. She ended up hiring someone, only to find—even after checking multiple references—that the person took off work repeatedly in the first couple of weeks on the job without any notice. Sarah would walk into the office expecting to see her, and then hours later would get an e-mail saying she wasn't coming in! It was discovered later that the woman had also lied about her excuse. Kevin, on the other hand, always reaches out to his LifeNet, through friends from school, whether for an employee, partner, or other resource. In fact, he's part of a network group of like-minded people that allows him to send out requests for special needs. It's how Kevin has found several key people, from his designer to his partner, a doctor. Can you see how, in the end, Kevin probably found more qualified people? He could also feel better about his decisions because the people referred to him came from like-minded people. Kevin's network is, in essence, prescreening the job candidates for him, whereas Sarah, who didn't use her LifeNet, spent more time scouring applicants online, and ultimately hired the wrong person, wasting precious time.

In general, reaching out to all levels of your LifeNet when making personnel decisions can pay enormous dividends. Not only will you get better information, but at some point the people you contact will reach out to *you* for feedback. It's that kind of reciprocity that will continue to feed your LifeNet.

More Hot Tips

- **Keep an Open Mind.** Approach each new contact or experience as if the next will change your life. It just might.
- **When in Doubt, Ask!** If you don't ask, you will never receive from your Home Zone. People don't know what you want if you don't tell them. If you never mention to your boss that you're eager to move up, if you never offer to take on additional work, if you seem happy to stay where you are, it's a sure bet you won't get promoted.
- **Segment Your Home Zone.** Put your marketing hat on before you call. Know who's good at what and what kind of value they can add. Do you need someone with particular industry knowledge? Do you need someone who understands marketing or technology? Sometimes just having someone with business experience and a wide streak of common sense to bounce ideas off of works wonders. Create an informal advisory board to help with everything from reviewing resumes to double checking budgets to cleaning viruses off your computers.

QUICK TIP: Creating a Personal Advisory Board from Your Home Zone

You can create your own Advisory Board to help you in any number of ways. Here's how to do it:

- Identify needs: Think about what expertise you need that you don't have. Computers? Writing? Marketing?
- Review Home Zone: Look at the people you identified in Chapter 3, in your Home Zone. Who can fill your needs?

Who might know of someone who can help you, such as a retired executive, business owner, or former colleague?
- Pick the Best: Once you've identified candidates, meet with them to talk about your venture or project. They need to be knowledgeable, willing and, most important, available.
- Give Back: Be alert to ways to help your advisers in return. Don't expect them to ask. By developing a relationship with them, you'll naturally encounter ways to reciprocate.

Put Your Home Zone to Work

Whether you're working for a company or running your own business, chances are your Home Zone can help you right now. Let's stop and think how. Start with this exercise.

Exercise: Read through the following situations and think about who in your Home Zone you could reach out to for support in each situation.

- You need some feedback for an idea you have for an investment opportunity.
- You're feeling discouraged by a recent setback and need someone to give you a little perspective and boost your spirits.
- You need a referral to a good CPA.
- You want to improve your salary, or your prospects for promotion, by getting hired at a particular company.
- You have an idea for a real-estate development opportunity and need a second opinion.
- Your business has expanded beyond your expectations and you need to hire one or two people to assist with the day-to-day operations.
- You've done a great job managing inventory but you need someone to help organize your general ledger and help you improve your budgetary process.

- Sales for your product have really picked up and you need another injection of capital if you're going to keep up with demand.
- You've written a marketing plan for your business and you'd like someone to review it before you invest any money.

Now let's take it a step further. List three specific ways your Home Zone—people, places, and resources—can help you right now to generate more income. I gave you a few examples earlier, such as serving as an informal adviser or giving you a referral to a reputable attorney who can help protect your assets or even getting feedback on a new business idea.

List three ways that members of your Home Zone can help you build your wealth:

Person/Place   *How They Can Help*

1. _____   _____

2. _____   _____

3. _____   _____

Find Success in Your Home Zone

Let's look at another success story, this one about a woman who found financial fulfillment at home. See whether you can glean the two distinct ways she tapped her Home Zone to find financial success.

Norma and Steve are an average couple who commuted to their jobs from the suburbs near New York City, not particularly satisfied with the direction their lives had taken, but too busy and stressed out to have time to even think about making a change.

One day while she was working out at the gym, Norma noticed a woman wearing a bright metallic disk taped to her elbow.

"It's a therapeutic magnet," the woman explained. "It's done wonders for my tennis elbow. You should try it."

Norma, who suffered from chronic knee pain, took a magnet

home. For three days she wore it on her knee. Amazingly, the pain disappeared. Astonished, Norma called the woman to see where she could buy some more. But the woman had borrowed it from a friend who had moved out of town.

Norma did some research online and discovered the name of the Scandinavian company which manufactured the magnets, but their Web site was not geared for consumers. So she e-mailed the sales department to ask for help. Not long after, she got back a response.

It turned out the products are distributed by individuals working out of their homes, similar to Avon or Mary Kay. Since the company was new to the U.S. market, there were no distributors in Norma's area. Investigating further, she discovered it required very little capital to become a distributor, so she signed up to start selling in her geographical territory.

Norma then began, through word of mouth—first with her friends, then her health-club contacts, and finally health-care professionals and business contacts—to build the business. In fact, the neighborhood club where she first encountered the magnets turned out to be her biggest source of business.

So, I asked you earlier whether you could figure out the two ways Norma tapped her Home Zone. Any ideas?

First, Norma borrowed from her own experience with her personal health issue. She realized that if *she* felt that much better after wearing the disk, then it was highly likely that others would benefit as well. Second, Norma used her neighborhood health club as ground zero to start selling her product, ultimately proving its success.

The End Zone

When you begin to think about making money, redefining your Comfort Zone (as we discussed in the previous chapter) and putting your particular talents to work, you need to feel like you're still in your backyard. That is, you need to focus on the people, places, and resources in your Home Zone. Why? There are a slew of reasons.

- Opportunities are often close to home. You spend so much of your time and energy in the same, tightly knit groups, this is where you are bound to come across ideas, information, and introductions—as well as practical, financial, and emotional support.
- The people in your Home Zone are usually eager to see you succeed. That's invaluable support when you're moving toward the Millionaire Zone.
- Failing to use your Home Zone will cause you to expend more energy, time, money, and resources than necessary—and will hinder your chances for success.
- Your chances for success increase greatly when you focus on familiar ground. Working with what's known makes you more efficient by reducing your stress level. Remember, you're changing your old Comfort Zone by, perhaps, foregoing a regular paycheck, or trying to make a living on what used to be just a hobby.
- You're more self-assured when you stick to things you know. Remember how Wayne Finkel said he felt? He felt confident because he stayed "close to home" when he quit his day job. His venture was based on services he knew well and people he knew from his job.

When Dorothy finally awakens, at the finale of *The Wizard of Oz*, to discover that after all her wondrous, sometimes frightening, imaginary travels, she had been home in bed the whole time, it of course shows a more ironic truth. We often spend so much effort trying to find our path in strange places well beyond our experience, yet it's when we stay close to home that we finally discover ourselves. In a sense, Dorothy showed us that "the heart is where the *home* is"! And for reaching the Millionaire Zone, there's no place like the Home Zone.

· 6 ·

Key 4: From Passions to Profits

We've talked a lot about relying on the people and resources you know well when you start taking the steps to reach your financial goals. But there's one key that's really all about you and you alone.

I'm talking about what drives you. I call these passions your personal drivers. These are the activities and situations that excite you, that make you want to get up off the couch and *do something*. There's probably no more powerful way to turn a profit than to focus your energy on the things you love to do.

Let's face it: Moving to financial success takes time and energy. If you're not doing something that you're passionate about, it's going to be that much harder to overcome the hurdles that we inevitably face when making changes in our lives.

You'll have some fun in this chapter, because you'll get to look at the various things you love to do and re-consider them as possible money-making ventures. In my research, according to Harris Interactive, 74% of employed Americans say they want to learn how to turn their passions into profitable ventures, but don't know how to do it. In this chapter, I'll show you the strategies you need to be successful.

I'll also help you figure out which of your passions are likeliest to succeed, as well as how to set and reach goals to make it all happen. But first, for a little inspiration, read Marnie Walker's story.

Marnie's Story

Remember Marnie? At 17 and in high school, Marnie Walker had a bad fall. For eight years after that, she could not walk properly. Her doctors discovered that she had a bone disorder. It was an experience she'd take with her right into the business world and into making her first million.

"I went from captain of the cheerleading squad to people being afraid to approach me because I couldn't walk and my hair was falling out," she says. "And when I got out of the hospital, I just couldn't believe my friends wouldn't talk to me."

Marnie never forgot that feeling. Years later, in her mid-thirties, when she was working for a telecommunications company, Marnie began to have the same thoughts we've all probably had. "It's difficult for an employee to create wealth quickly. I want to give it a try—to start my own business."

Through a conversation with members of her LifeNet, Marnie got started in a venture that would change her life forever. One day Marnie was talking with some members of the local school board. The school officials were complaining about how difficult it was to get transportation for special-needs children, kids in wheelchairs and with disabilities. Marnie understood this issue all too well. After all, she had been a special-needs child for eight years.

"I was the same person inside, but you're treated very different on the outside," she says. "So I realized that if you understood what the issues were with these kids, you could transport them without having to deal with all the complaints of the other bus companies."

This was a venture Marnie felt passionate about—so passionate that even though "it wasn't enough to live on," she still pursued it. She stayed at her current job full-time until she could get a business plan together. Through other LifeNet connections, she managed to reach the right person at the bank to secure financing. The school board awarded her a contract to begin with eight buses for the first year. She started small, turning a bedroom into an office before renting what she describes as a "dump office over a retail strip mall."

Marnie's passion—trickling down to the bus drivers and into the homes of those children—was perhaps the single most important ingredient to her success. It was that personal commitment that ultimately enabled her to build a bus transportation company—called Student Express—with 250 buses generating over $10 million in annual sales.

"People got infected with my passion and that's huge," she says. "That's how I got the contract and raised the money from banks."

Marnie lived her dream and empowered employees to do the same. She had a bus driver's license and would hop in the buses on days when drivers were short. When the school board refused to let her stop buses in a congested area to drop off kids, she enlisted ideas from her drivers to get around the bureaucracy.

"One of the drivers said, 'Why don't we just call up the parents or ring the doorbell and introduce ourselves and tell them what time we'll be dropping their child off?' So we sent letters of introduction from drivers. We actually encouraged them to start a relationship with the parents. It became the best transportation the school ever had."

It's no surprise that parents wrote letters and voiced their appreciation at school board meetings for a transportation system that cared about their kids. It's also no surprise that Marnie's contracts with the school board kept getting bigger and more profitable as a result.

Example from the Millionaire Zone
Martha Stewart, chief executive, Martha Stewart Living
    Omnimedia
No. 377 on Forbes 400
Net worth: $970 million
Key strategy: From Passions to Profits

Martha Stewart is a shining example of the key strategy of turning passion into profits. The chef and home-décor maven started cooking and gardening as a very young girl. Her father was an avid gardener, and her mother and grandparents taught her how to bake and how to can and preserve fruits and vegetables. As a young woman, she did venture into other careers—she took modeling jobs to get through college, then worked in a brokerage firm for a while—but eventually, she returned to her original love: cooking and home décor. After she and her husband remodeled their 1805 Connecticut farmhouse into her well-known signature home, Martha Stewart began a catering business out of the basement. It quickly grew into a multimillion dollar enterprise that has since branched out into books, a magazine, a television show, and more. She's been quoted as saying, "All the things I love are what my business is all about."

CHAPTER CHECK-IN: How Marnie Turned Her Passion into Profits

- Personal experience as a teen instilled a sense of passion for those treated differently due to special needs
- Was able to demonstrate passion and commitment to key decision makers: school board members and bankers
- Maintained direct involvement in the business rather than staying "behind the desk," keeping her in touch with the business's needs
- Put responsibility in the hands of bus drivers to find creative solutions, which ultimately strengthened her company's relationships with parents and the school district

How Marine Reached the Millionaire Zone

- Learned of a need for better children's transportation through local LifeNet members on the school board
- Stayed in her full-time job to pay bills while building her business

- Received a year-long contract for eight buses, providing guaranteed income to support a loan
- Leveraged LifeNet members to get a bank loan to purchase buses
- Sold her $10 million per year business as the sole owner

What's a Personal Driver?

You can see how Marnie's passion set her and her company apart, and allowed her to push her company to the top of the ranks. I call that kind of passion a personal driver. I define personal drivers as those internal qualities that motivate you to do things differently and with more focus and energy than anyone else. Think about how you go about your life outside of work, doing things you enjoy, pursuing your interests. What are you passionate about?

One friend told me, "You know it's your passion if, when you're doing it, you lose all track of time." It's whatever gets your juices going, makes you excited to get up in the morning, helps you feel like the headaches are worth the cause—you get the idea.

Marnie Walker and many others profiled in this book converted a personal experience, and the passion aroused by that experience, into a launching pad for entry into the Zone. You can do the same. It's a common assertion that to have a fulfilling career, business, or life, you need to follow your passion, or in the words of Joseph Campbell, follow your bliss. The tough part is figuring out what your passion is, but first let's look at the powerful benefits your personal drivers can bring to your venture.

➤ FAST FACTS: What Is Passion?

1. A powerful emotion, such as love, joy, hatred, or anger
2. Boundless enthusiasm: *His skills as a player don't quite match his passion for the game.*
3. The object of such enthusiasm: *Soccer is her passion.*

Source: *American Heritage Dictionary*

Passion Power

Mark Fitzgerald, the shoe retailer we talked about in Chapter 4, says, "If you don't have passion, you're going to lack that extra something that gives you an edge." Mark says he and his partner go head-to-head with competitors every day who are not passionate about the business they're in. Mark says that sets his company apart. "We hear from people all the time, 'You guys love what you do and we love what you do for us.' It makes a big difference."

Your passion can improve the service or product you deliver, and passion can give you the edge with competitors. As Mark points out, why would anyone want to work with someone who's *not* passionate when they have the option of working with someone who *is* passionate? It's clear that people like Mark will go the extra mile to get the job done. Passion is what will keep you getting up every day, pushing and prodding to make your dream a reality.

Passion can also make the difference in your ability to persuade, to get what you want. Consider 33-year-old Jason Jiang. A young entrepreneur in China, he decided the best way for advertisers to reach customers was to sell ads on electronic billboards in office-building lobbies. In desperate need of start-up cash for his novel idea, he went to a private-equity firm and spoke intensely about his business strategy, not leaving out the potential downsides of his business model. Finally, he said he would personally share the risks he was asking investors to make, according to a *Wall Street Journal* article describing the meeting. What was the result of Jiang's passion and willingness to risk his own personal wealth? The venture capitalist promised $12 million. Jiang had asked for a little more than $6 million.

There are many ways to reach investors for your venture. I talked earlier about the role of friends and family. But if you're raising a large amount of money or you're on your second round of capital, consider current or retired executives in the industry, angel investor groups, venture capital firms, or companies that might have an interest in using your product or service. You can find out about many of these groups through a simple online search ("angel investor group" or "venture capital firms") or often by connecting with people through your LifeNet. Just remember that passion, as Jiang discovered, can make all the difference.

When Two Passions Meet

Stuart and Stephanie Liner are another example of turning passion into profits. They vaulted into the Millionaire Zone almost by accident: Thanks to some money he earned as a lawyer, they were able to buy a house and fix it up, with Stephanie serving as everything from general contractor to interior designer. Soon after they were done, someone walked up to their front door and offered them more than $2 million for the house. Ever since, thanks to Stephanie's passion to "build a nest," as Stuart puts it, they've been able to fix up homes and make much more money than they'd make relying only on his income as a lawyer. Since then, Stuart and Stephanie have purchased, restored, and sold more than a dozen houses, generating over $50 million in real estate sales in seven years! Before they started, they never realized the degree to which others would respond to Stephanie's passion for good design.

QUICK TIP: The Power of Passion

Your personal drivers provide some valuable benefits:

- Your product/service becomes better—Marnie's bus transportation company knew what to offer parents, kids, and school districts to make her company stand out.
- Your customers prefer you over competitors—as Mark shows us, anyone would prefer to work with someone who has passion for what they do.
- You become more persuasive—when you believe in something

so strongly, it's impossible *not* to be convincing. That's how Jason Jiang got into the Millionaire Zone.

* You endure during tough times—when you have a vivid sense of the "rightness" of what you're doing, it helps you see that rough times, such as slow business or rejection—aren't a reflection of you, your self-worth, or the worth of your project. After all, you know how valuable and important your product or service is!

CHAPTER CHECK-IN: *Three Ingredients for a Profitable Venture*

We've talked about passion. There are two more ingredients you need to combine with your passion: Skills and knowledge. We'll discuss those in this section.

* Passion
* Skills
* Knowledge

From Passion to Purchase

When you're passionate about something, it can inspire others to feel passionate as well. If you combine that passion with a need, the end result is buying behavior.

It looks like this:

Passion + Need —➤ Inspiration —➤ Buying Decision

Think about it. Maybe you watch those home makeover shows. Aren't you more inspired to go fix up your own home when you see the passion behind some of those talk show hosts? Their passion almost makes you feel you need to improve your home.

You're then inspired to walk into some home improvement store, which then leads you buy those nifty shelves for the kid's room or the paint and sponges for a new but affordable look on the walls. Yes, your passion alone can truly drive people into certain behaviors.

Two More Ingredients: Skills & Knowledge

But there are some other key ingredients to this recipe for turning passion into profits. Let's use a car as an analogy. Your passion is the gas. It's what keeps the car going every day, all year long, rain or shine, hot or cold. The inspiration is what the car looks like. It makes others go "Ooh . . . ahh! I like that!"

But do you know how to drive the car? Besides passion, you also need skills and knowledge. You can think of skills as "do you know *how* to drive the car?" Meanwhile, knowledge is "do you know *where* you're going?"

Without the passion, the car won't go anywhere. Without the skills, you'll crash quickly. Without the knowledge, you'll get lost. It's all got to be working together. Let's talk about skills and knowledge in a bit more depth.

Skills are a combination of knowledge, expertise, and talent. For instance, the ability to make jewelry, restore a car, and manage other people's finances are all particular skills. You might have skills working with others, skills with numbers, or mechanical skills.

Any venture will require a variety of skills to keep it going and push it to success. But that doesn't mean a lack of any one skill should stop you from moving forward: Your LifeNet is there to help you shore up any deficiencies.

Then there's knowledge. To make money over the long haul, you need to know what you're getting into. You need to know the landscape of that particular industry. You need to know the basics. At the very least, you need to know where you can go to learn the basics.

Test Your Passion

You need to feel passionate about your endeavor to be successful. But that doesn't mean that everything you feel passionate about will be able to move you into the Millionaire Zone.

To test each of your personal passions, answer the following three questions. The answers to these questions will help you determine whether that particular passion has the necessary characteristics to propel you to the Zone, or whether it's best as an enjoyable hobby.

Does your passion inspire others? That is, do others see it as a valuable undertaking, a worthwhile endeavor, an exciting possibility? If you're passionate about what you're doing, but others don't share that feeling, you're likely to hit roadblocks early on.

Does your passion fulfill a need? In other words, do people want what you make or create from your passion? For example, if you love jewelry and create your own, do your friends ask you where you bought that great necklace? Here's an example from my life. I'm passionate about working with people to improve their financial lives. But my passion alone isn't enough. If there weren't a real need for financial education in this country, I could not be successful.

Do you want to take it to a higher level? That is, you have to want to really push further and further with this passion. You need to be able to set achievable goals for the future. For instance, maybe you love making jewelry, but you don't want to do it more than an hour or two a week. Or do you want to quit your job and do jewelry full-time? Do you want to walk into a Bloomingdale's and see your jewelry? Or, you love rebuilding your 1966 Shelby Mustang, but you love it because it's an escape from work—you wouldn't want to do it all the time. Some passions are meant to remain hobbies. Others can be harnessed into something bigger. If you can see yourself restoring one Mustang after another, you might have a new venture on your hands!

To answer these questions about your personal drivers, you need to write down all of the various things you love to do, and figure out which passions have the potential to be something bigger.

Exercise: Write a list of all the things you're passionate about, no matter how trivial.

_____

_____

_____

_____

_____

_____

_____

_____

_____

_____

Now what are your skills and knowledge, and how do they relate to your passions?

Exercise: Take a look at the list of your passions. Narrow it down to five passions, and complete the following checklist for each.

Your Passions and Your Skills

Passions	Example					
(Write your passions in each box to the right.)	Flowers					
Do I have the skills?	Yes—I make arrangements that friends rave about.					
Do I have the knowledge?	Yes—I worked in a flower shop.					

Reality Check

Now that you've listed your passions and any related skills and knowledge, go back and double-check. Ask yourself, "Is that really what I'm most passionate about?" Do the same for skills and knowledge: "Are those truly the skills and knowledge I have?" Your best enterprise will involve something that combines your passions with the best of your skills and knowledge.

Elaine Floyd is a great example of someone who combines her passion with skills and knowledge. Elaine was a stockbroker who discovered that she had a talent for writing about complicated financial concepts in a way that made them easily understood. She decided to leave the brokerage industry to pursue her passion for writing. But rather than go off in a completely different direction and pursue, say, creative fiction writing, she chose to tap the skills and knowledge she'd gained from her career in the brokerage business and base her writing career around financial topics. Elaine is now a successful freelance financial writer and has written countless books and articles. Her success is driven by her passion for writing combined with her ability (skills and knowledge) to educate people about the business she knows best.

Keep in mind that you don't need to have an exhaustive knowledge of the area you're passionate about. But before you devote more time and money to it, you'll need to gain that knowledge. Completing the skills and knowledge exercise above is a surefire way of clarifying what you know and don't know before you take your next step on the path to the Millionaire Zone. Don't forget that in Chapter 12, I'll take you through a more detailed, 30-day program to help you turn those passions into profits.

Bridge Gaps with Your LifeNet

Now, take another look at the list you've just created. Are there some gaps in your skills and knowledge boxes? Well, we all have strengths and weaknesses. What separates the winners from everyone else is that they know their strengths and weaknesses. They know precisely what they do well and where they need help.

You need to be honest with yourself about your weaknesses. By identifying them early, you can be on the lookout for someone with complementary assets that can offset whatever you're missing. This is where your LifeNet can play a really powerful role.

Say you've got a great idea for a new venture, but you don't have the accounting and organizational skills necessary to manage the accounts receivable and payables. Or maybe you don't have the technical skills needed to build a great Web site. Mark, our entrepreneur from Chapter 4, sure didn't have contacts in the shoe industry when he began his venture, but tapping into his LifeNet paid off.

"Talking to people we knew was critical, having not been in the industry before," he says. "One of my partners had worked for a retailer a while back, so we started talking to them. They really got us started in terms of supplies. They not only had a retail business, but wholesale as well, so we also got our shoes from them. It's about leveraging who you know."

Make It Happen

We talked earlier about the power of thinking big. If you want to turn your passion into million-dollar profits, you need to think big. But you also need to set realistic goals.

Studies show that we're much more likely to achieve success if we write down our goals. Even in my own research for this book, we

found 77% of millionaires surveyed had a plan to make their money. Did you know that the vast majority of average Americans—some 73%, according to the Employee Benefit Research Institute—not only don't have a plan for making money, they haven't even calculated what they need to retire on?

Do you see a pattern? Those who want to get ahead set goals, and then work to meet them. They know you can't just sit back and hope it will happen. In other words, you don't need a map if you don't care where you're going. You *might* get lucky and get to a seven-figure fortune, but your chances for success improve dramatically if you do have goals.

Even as an employee, setting goals for your own success will work wonders. It will keep you focused on what matters when the daily minutiae threaten to eat up your time. It will give you concrete goals to share with your boss and others. It will give you clear examples of your accomplishments—a hero report as I call it—that you can use to move up in your current company, go somewhere else, or start your own venture. You can use that list of the goals you've set and achieved as the basis of your request for a promotion or raise. Or that list can form the heart of your resume and pitch to a prospective employer. Or you can use it to describe yourself in your pitch to investors or lenders.

I set goals every year as part of my annual plan. And I review them regularly. But I also set goals for shorter time frames: daily, weekly, monthly. It keeps me focused and gives me a sense of accomplishment every day. It also ensures I use my time efficiently.

In my research, I found that of those millionaires who did develop a plan, fully 82% created one with a five-year time horizon—or longer! That's also consistent with the strategic planning of most larger companies. But you'll also want to set shorter-term, say, one-year goals, to give you ways to measure how successful you are in moving toward the Millionaire Zone.

Visualize Your Goals

You know you have some goals, but what are they *exactly?* In this section, we use Robert Caulfield's business as an example of the specific ways you need to think about your goals for the future.

Robert is trying to turn his passion into profits. He's got a business going that generates $100,000 a year on the side by selling chewable dog treats that freshen dogs' breath. But he wants to take it further. He set goals to grow his business 30% each year, which would take him to generating almost $360,000 annually in five years. Not bad. But by setting more goals and thinking bigger, Robert can take it further.

First, Robert needs to step back and visualize his business. What ultimately can this business become? The leader in dog-breath treats? The leader in all dog treats? The leader in online sales of dog treats? The most recognized brand for dog-breath treats? How about cat-breath treats? Visualize what your venture will look like in five years. That image will be with you all the time, and it'll help you communicate that passion for your dream in a way you hadn't before. Having that mental picture also helps you avoid distractions, and keeps you moving toward making your vision a reality. I've done it—and believe me it works.

Second, Robert needs to set goals to help him achieve his dream. I like to suggest creating goals for each year up to five years. What goals do you need to accomplish to keep you on track to reach your first-year goal? What kind of goals could Robert set to boost his business more than 30% and get him closer to the Millionaire Zone? He could test some online sales or try distributing his product through partners, like other companies in the pet space. Just one successful partner or new marketing test could easily boost his sales. If he can double his sales to $200,000 and keep up a 30% annual growth rate, he'll be at over $700,000 annually in five years.

Other possible goals for Robert are to hire a sales person or, if cash is tight, partner-up with an online marketing firm and share the profits rather than paying an employee out-of-pocket.

Bob Lorsch is a wildly successful entrepreneur who understands the power of visualization. When just a young man starting out selling smokeless cigarettes, his goal was to make $100 a day. Well, he reached that goal—and surpassed it. Today, his goal is to turn www.mymedicalrecords.com into a billion-dollar company that helps address an important need.

By visualizing what you want your passion to become and then setting goals to get there, you'll turbo-charge your chances of success.

The End Zone

Passion is the one thing you won't get from someone else. In fact, it's all internal and it differs for everyone. It's the only component completely dependent on you. Passion drives all entrepreneurs and most successful people. You can't achieve anything significant without passion.

Why is passion important?

- When you are truly passionate and in touch with your drivers, persistence and commitment automatically follow. Without them, you won't make it to the Zone. Every financially successful person I've ever met or interviewed for this book demonstrated persistence and commitment.
- Passion can make the difference in your success because it creates stronger connections with your customers and other business contacts.
- Passion gives you an extra edge over your competitors because it makes you more persuasive and keeps you going when times get tough.
- Remember, though, you need to assess whether the things you love to do might be your ticket to the Millionaire Zone, and to match your passion with your skills and knowledge.

As we leave this topic, let me share just one more story with you.

Ron Greitzer has a passion for cleaning up the environment. In fact, he transformed that passion into a carpet-recycling business that today recycles 100 million pounds of waste carpet—enough to fill the Rose Bowl three times! His excitement about what he's doing made it possible for him to get through the hard times that all businesses inevitably face.

"When business is tough, I still wake up with a big smile on my face knowing I'm doing something for society," Ron says. "The benefits aren't only financial.

"I've always wanted to make a difference," he adds. "Doing the volume of recycling that we do is making a big difference to our community and our nation. I just received Recycle Person of the Year."

Key 5: Make 'Em Want It

In earlier chapters, we talked about the key strategies of identifying your personal drivers, understanding your Home Zone, and building your LifeNet. But if no one *wants* your product, service, or particular skill set, obviously, it will be impossible to grow your business or move forward in your career. That's why it's essential to use your LifeNet to test your drivers—the particular passions that make you tick—against the demands of the real world.

How do you do that? You test demand for your product, service, idea, or skills using your LifeNet, and then create demand for it to ensure strong sales. You can test and create demand without losing money, and get people to want not just your product or service, but want you.

Erica's Story

Take a look at what Erica Zohar did to create demand. She's the mom in her mid-thirties, the one who's always loved clothes. These days Erica's clothing company, American Groove, is a success. But it wasn't always that way. She started smaller—much smaller—and she created demand for her product without throwing tons of money at it. Here's her story.

A few years ago, Erica was busy running her first business, which she had started while she was still in college, selling ads for student discount cards. It was a fun little business and she enjoyed it. She'd created it from scratch. It was fueled by her passion for good discount shopping, and she persuaded nine major universities in Florida and California to embrace the idea. But she felt hampered by the fact that demand was relatively limited: She could only sell a set number of retailer ads per card. Plus there was the uphill sales pitch of convincing retailers to shell out for the ads (plus a 10% discount) to bring in college kids. The retailers who bought into the program were good repeat customers, but getting that first sale wasn't easy. She had a decent business going, but she couldn't stop thinking about one of her real loves: clothes.

Erica had never been in the apparel business (unless you count the homemade elastic fabric hair ties she sold in high school!), but she knew what she liked. And, as a young working mom, she wanted comfortable yet fashionable sweats. The problem, back in the mid-1990s, was that "sweats" meant ugly workout pants. You didn't really want to be seen at a nice restaurant lunch in them. Erica couldn't find the comfortable yet chic look she wanted when she went shopping. So she started thinking she could design her own line of clothes.

"I had some ideas I thought would sell. It was right at the time when contemporary sportswear didn't have a niche yet. It was for the mom who picked up her kids at school and then went out to lunch. But it wasn't The Gap, it was more of a conversation piece. That's when my line came out," Erica says.

CHAPTER CHECK-IN: How Erica Made 'Em Want It

- Identified her own desire for trendy but comfortable clothes
- Confirmed demand for these clothes by talking to friends, others in her LifeNet
- Produced sample pieces and received feedback from friends via a small focus group
- Took samples to a major conference to test real-world demand

---

Example from the Millionaire Zone
Sam Walton, founder, Wal-Mart
Walton's heirs are Nos. 6, 7, 8, 9, and 10 on Forbes 400
Combined net worth of heirs to the Walton fortune: $77.9 billion
Key strategy: Make 'Em Want It

One sure-fire way to create demand for you—which is a key strategy in moving toward the kind of financial success you're looking for—is so simple you may not even believe me.

Here it is: Just be nice.

Find that hard to believe? Consider Sam Walton, founder of the retail behemoth Wal-Mart. From his youngest days in high school, through college and on into his business career, he made a point of being nice to the people he met.

Listen to what Walton said in an interview years ago, as he described trying to get elected to his college's student government, in the book *Masters of Enterprise*. "I learned early on that one of the secrets to campus leadership was the simplest thing of all: speak to people coming down the sidewalk before they speak to you. I would always look ahead and speak to the person coming toward me. If I knew them, I would call them by name, but even if I didn't, I would still speak to them. Before long, I probably knew more students than anybody in the university; and they recognized me and considered me their friend."

Years later, he founded his discount-store empire on that very idea. Wal-Mart stores are known for their friendliness. There are greeters, and they call every customer a friend. This stems from Walton's own friendly nature and the fact that he saw being friendly as a sure way to get ahead. He must have been right. Just look at the empire he built!

You've Got the Idea—What's Next?

Having read this far in this book, you can probably guess what Erica's first step was to making her dream a reality. That's right, she turned to her LifeNet.

She started telling her friends that she wanted to design her own line of clothes. One friend from college told her to call his sister, who worked for a clothing buyer for a major store.

Here's a perfect example of the power of your LifeNet. Erica's passion for designing clothes leads her to talk unabashedly to people about her idea. Before she knows it, she's discovered that one of those people had a sister who happened to be a buyer's representative—and that person was instrumental in getting Erica's business off the ground.

"She taught me in 24 hours how the business works," Erica says now, remembering that conversation. "You bring your stuff to a show, you get someone to rep your line, you write orders, you make it, you pack it, you ship it."

Did Erica, now armed with information on how the clothing business worked (Remember? Passion plus skills plus knowledge), take out an enormous bank loan, or mortgage her house to the hilt to get her venture going? No. She decided to make sure there was demand for her product first before she jumped in with both feet.

QUICK TIP: *Ways to Test Your Idea Affordably*

The last thing you want to do is blow all your money or mortgage your house without first testing your idea. Here's how to do it affordably:

- Make samples: Build a sample or prototype of your product or service. Take it to a trade show or directly to potential customers to get feedback—and orders.
- Conduct a homemade focus group: You can avoid spending large sums of money and get excellent feedback by conducting a small, in-person focus group made up of friends and acquaintances (your LifeNet!) who meet the definition of your target customer. A similar but potentially costly option is to pay a company to conduct a survey to assess demand.
- Call possible customers: Create a list of likely users of your product or service. Then, call and ask them if they would use the product or service if you were to create it.

Start Small

To keep her expenses low, Erica took some cash from her advertising business—$10,000 in all—to create samples of her clothing line.

"I thought back to my high school days, when I made and sold fabric hair ties. I remembered I had gone to a tailor, so I used that knowledge and went down the street and got my samples from the local tailor."

Talk about using your Home Zone and focusing on familiar territory! Not only did she access resources in her neighborhood, but she used an earlier experience in her life to solve her problem.

Did she ask the tailor to make a 100-piece clothing line? No. She kept things small, in test mode. "I asked him to make pants, shorts, a sweatshirt, a T-shirt, a tank, and a cropped sweatshirt. Six pieces," Erica says. Then she heard about a big clothing show taking place in New York, and found a woman willing to share the cost of a booth to exhibit at the show. "I literally split a 10-by-10 booth with her," Erica says.

So, what did Erica get back for her $10,000 investment?

At that clothing show, her first ever, with just six pieces in her clothing line, Erica wrote $45,000 worth of orders, including one from Bloomingdale's. Her total outlay, including paying the tailor for making the samples, flying to New York, and the cost of the booth was $10,000.

How Erica Reached the Millionaire Zone
- Decided how much she was willing to lose
- Surveyed friends in her LifeNet about her idea for stylish but comfortable clothes
- Learned about the buying process at retail stores through another LifeNet member
- Had sample clothing pieces created to get orders before spending money on producing more
- Shared a booth at a conference to keep costs low and secure her first $45,000 in orders
- Avoids disclosing specific revenue figures to maintain her company's national image—and prevent competitors from using information against her—though she generated $1.5 million in sales her first year
- Distributes to major retailers nationwide and has expanded line to include kids' clothes

Conduct a Homemade Focus Group

Another good idea is to use your LifeNet as a focus group. Make sure this group is comprised of your likely target buyers. For instance, Erica wouldn't talk to adults over 30 if she was going to create a line aimed at teens. Also, make sure your focus group is big enough to get some good and varied feedback (8 to 12 people is typical).

Erica says, "To this day, I have all my mom friends look at my designs. 'Is this cute? Would you wear that? Is that too young?'" For instance, she found out that "a lot of moms don't want the low-rise thing. They want it to look like it's low-rise, but not that young. I always use my friends. In exchange, they get free clothes."

Call Possible Customers

I remember recently when a good friend of mine, Karlyn Carnahan, came to me with a new business idea: a company that helps consumers, small businesses, and insurance companies plan and prepare for disasters such as hurricanes or earthquakes. She asked me to take a look at her plan and her sample Web site, which she created to pitch the idea to potential investors.

Her presentation was very impressive. But as I went through it, I was concerned about who would cover what costs and about her ability to make money. Then I remembered something she had told me, that she learned during her days working in the insurance industry.

Insurers pay hundreds of thousands of dollars for the kind of catastrophe information and tools her company would provide, only not nearly as robust as hers would be. I called Karlyn and said, "It seems to me the insurance companies are in the greatest need for your service." She agreed.

After we hung up, Karlyn did some online research and found that, in fact, a new law had been proposed which would *require* insurance companies to provide certain information and services related to catastrophes. This new law would certainly drive demand for her online venture. She was elated to have discovered this important industry change.

I also gave her another important suggestion. "Karlyn, look, if you really want to raise money to build this company, why don't you pick up the phone to the top-ten insurance companies and see if they're interested?"

"Gosh," she exclaimed, "why didn't I think of that?" By showing her mock-up to insurance companies, including her previous employer, and getting verbal commitments, Karlyn could demonstrate demand. She could then go back to investors with a list of the companies with whom she had met and their level of interest and financial commitment.

QUICK TIP: *When You Call Potential Customers, Consider These Tips*

When you call prospective customers, partners, or anyone else as you're testing the waters, you'll want to follow this advice:

- Use your LifeNet to get a referral. If you can, you'll have a better chance of getting to the right person.
- Have your questions ready. Be organized so you can get all the information you need; don't assume you'll be able to go back and ask additional questions.
- Be mindful of other people's time. Promise to keep their time to ten minutes, long enough to present your information but not too much to take them away from their priorities.

Become a Client to Your Employer

Here's a powerful notion to consider as you start testing the market for demand. Why not make your employer your first client? I know it sounds a little intimidating—telling your boss you want to quit so you can sell him a product—but stop and think about it. When you leave that "safe" corporate job for your new venture, there's no reason you shouldn't consider lining up orders from your former employer and making your transition a smoother one. After all, becoming a vendor should be much more palatable to your boss than becoming a competitor.

These days, your employer is likely to consider your suggestion. Many companies are looking for ways to outsource tasks. Remember how I talked earlier about companies taking jobs overseas and looking for ways to cut health-care costs? Well, outsourcing is a way for them to reduce those costs, especially since employee benefits alone add a whopping 30% on average to a person's salary. If you've been at a company that has started outsourcing, consider going to your boss with a proposal before your boss comes to you with a pink slip.

Let's say you're a medical transcriber (someone who types up physicians' notes about their patients) for a cardiologist near a major hospital. You're tired of schlepping into the office, although you like your job. You have the idea of continuing to work as a transcriber, but doing it from home. You hook up with an online recording software company where the physician can use his PC to dictate right online.

Then you tell the doctor you can set up a Web site for him so he can use his phone to dictate his notes. You get the raw transcript, clean it up, and e-mail it to him overnight. Now, you know the hospital is trying to cut costs. Once you've got your system perfected, you go to the hospital administrator with a plan. Before the end of the year, you have 30 physicians paying $2,000 a month and now you're making $720,000 a year and staying at home. And your former employer was your first client. You are on your way to the Millionaire Zone.

Whether it's medical transcribing or something else, you know your job better than anyone. You know what your clients are looking for, both your "clients" within and outside the company. You believe you can deliver a product or service to those customers better than your employer does. And now you have the freedom to be your own boss and make your own decisions—and make more money.

QUICK TIP: Turn Your Employer into a Customer

Approaching your employer as your next customer might feel intimidating. Here's how to do it:

- Create a plan: Either a formal business plan or a sample of the product so they can see the level of your seriousness and "touch and feel" the product or service.

* Do your homework: Who are other potential clients? Get feedback from peers and other relevant people at your current or ex-employer to make sure you've got a compelling product or service that will address their need.
* Go to the decision-maker: Remember, if you want the business, ask the person who can say yes.

QUICK TIP: Starting Out: Act Bigger than You Are

You might face the inevitable Catch-22 when you're starting out of needing to sound big when in fact you're not. Here's my advice:

* Keep in mind that perceptions matter. "Half the battle is perception," says Erica Zohar. "People want to give their money to people they feel are going to do something with it. They feel a lot more comfortable if they feel there are more people involved. It's a pretty powerful distinction."
* Talk in the plural. When starting out and trying to create demand for your product or business, talk in the plural. Instead of saying "I've got this great widget," say "*We're* producing this great widget."
* Avoid negatives. If your sales or volume is small, don't get into specifics. Instead, as Erica suggests, talk about goals: "This year, we plan to serve X number of customers" or "do X amount of business."

Developing Ideas for In-Demand Products or Services

Are you out of ideas? Confused on where to start? You know you've got skills, knowledge, passion, but none of those attributes seems to translate into real world opportunities. You're saying to yourself, "Help me think of great ideas."

No problem! It's easier than you think. Ask yourself about demand around you—what are the things that drive you crazy? For instance, cell phones that don't work well, or long lines at the bank. These are the problems that lead to direct improvements.

Don't forget there's always room to build on earlier innovations, so don't think that someone's already been there and done that. Consider how the low-fat craze drove demand for low-fat products, but then the lack of a good tasting low-fat product led to someone creating a tastier cookie.

I've wondered for years why there was no bank open all day on Saturdays, when I actually have time to go, or why there's a Starbucks for coffee drinkers but nothing devoted to tea drinkers. Every concept in business started with a question: "Why hasn't someone . . . ?"

You can see demand right in your own LifeNet, even without reading the paper or having a personal complaint. For instance, when you go to a party, listen. What do you hear people talking about? Investing in real estate in a slowing market, perhaps? Or starting to use some new cheap Internet phone service they read about in an industry publication? Start thinking about your personal drivers and how they might play into the needs of those around you.

Exercise: List three examples of demand you see around you now. Look to newspapers and magazines. Listen to the radio and watch TV. Watch the world around you as you're out. I'll get you started:

- On an unexpectedly rainy day, you'll see everyone (including you) without an umbrella, but now forced to buy one. An idea could be for an automatic umbrella dispenser where people can buy disposable umbrellas really cheaply without feeling like they're getting ripped off by vendors charging $20.
- I drive through towns and see a lot of development going on. That tells me the lot for sale next door might be in demand in the near future, so if I buy now I might be able to make a nice profit.

- I'm in a resort community looking at real estate. As I'm waiting for my broker to get ready to show me property, I overhear another broker mentioning that Moxie Java, a growing regional coffee retailer, is coming soon. That tells me there will likely be even more demand for property.

Now, list three examples of demand happening around you.

1. _____

2. _____

3. _____

Exercise: Think about the personal drivers you defined in the last chapter and how you can create demand for them in order to identify viable opportunities.

On a piece of paper, write each of your personal drivers at the top. Along the side, list the elements in your Home Zone. Then think about the ways each element in your Home Zone may have demand for your personal driver. It will look something like the table on the next page.

Make 'Em Want It

Now that you've got the tools to test your idea to see that *some* demand exists, I want to talk about creating more demand. You see, so many people starting out don't understand the power of creating demand. When I say *create demand*, I mean making lots of people really want your product. This is as important at the earliest point in the game, just after you've tested your idea, as it is later, when your venture is up and making money. And don't forget, if your focus is on advancing your career in the corporate world, these same strategies will help you be more successful and increase your chances of a promotion.

Some people may not even *know* they want your (or your company's) product or service. Creating demand can be about generating

Personal Drivers	Carpentry	Interior Design	Real-estate Investing	Animals
Family			Dad needs a new investment opportunity and can help fund my real-estate ventures.	
Friends		Friend Suzi needs help desperately! Her walls are bare and her furniture is mismatched. "House calls" could be an in-home interior design service.		
Neighbors				A "pet store on wheels" could bring animals and needed products into the neighborhood.
School	Kids need modular furniture. Develop line of modular furniture.			

a buying behavior almost out of thin air! I'm sure whoever designed the VW Beetle never started out assuming that people would demand a small ugly German-made car, but by creating an image of cuteness, durability, dependability, and economy, the Bug became one of the best-selling cars of all time.

No matter what, if you can create demand, you will grow faster, make more money, reach your goals sooner and, if you're like me, have the best time of your life.

Creating Demand Where There Is None

This sounds crazy: How can you create demand when no demand exists? *Jennifer*, you must be thinking, *what in the world are you talking about?* Listen, was there any demand for *Big Mouth Billy Bass* before we saw it on TV? Well, few could have anticipated the demand; there certainly was no obvious need for it. But that didn't mean that no one wanted to buy it once they saw it. They did! That fish was one of the biggest-selling novelty items in marketing history.

And remember the Pet Rock craze in the 1970s? No one knew they needed to spend almost $4 on a rock before advertising man Gary Dahl pitched the idea, an idea he came up with one night while hanging out with some buddies. He created demand to the tune of almost $4 million in a few short months. That amazes me—that a *rock* generated that much money. Look, if the creator of that product can create that kind of demand and that kind of money, so can you.

Did you ever think, walking around your neighborhood 10 years ago, that you needed another *coffee* shop? Of course not. Today there's hardly a neighborhood corner without a Starbucks.

How did founder and CEO Howard Schultz get started? He worked in a coffee shop, developed a passion for the business, and came to know and understand the operation. He then had a vision for the store—remember how vital it is to have a vision, a plan— and ended up buying that very store to turn it into his reality.

Thanks to high profit margins on coffee and an ability to create an attractive store where people would want to hang out (even take dates!), Howard was able to expand from just one store to 10,000 coffee shops in 30 countries, with a company valued at over $6 billion. Today Schultz is worth $700 million.

Just because you may not at first see or feel demand doesn't mean there is not demand for your idea. Go ahead and test. The "need" for your business may not be obvious, but if the initial responses are positive, there are ways to keep the momentum going.

CHAPTER CHECK-IN: *Ways to Create Real Demand*

In this section, we look at three ways to create demand:

* Create competition.
* Generate buzz.
* Make people demand you.

Create Competition

When I say to create competition, I mean getting more than one person to want you, your idea, or your product. The more people who want you—or who *appear* to want you—the more in demand you'll be. It's the herd mentality.

Here's a great example. In the venture capital (VC) world—the world of professionals who invest in young companies in exchange for ownership—you'll see this herd mentality run rampant. It's what led so many VC firms to invest in unproven technologies during the dot-com era. There was such a rush for IPO gold, that one VC firm would follow whatever another one was doing.

Here's how this psychology can work to your advantage. Let's say Nelson goes to an investor conference to drum up interest in his Internet-based natural herbal supplement company. This conference takes place right after his three other meetings with potential investors in the last two days. An investor at the conference asks the inevitable question: "Who else is interested in your company?" Now Nelson can say, "I've just met with three investor groups over the last two days and they're keenly interested." The investor, obviously, shows greater interest in the project. He thinks to himself, "Well, if *they're* interested, this must be a good opportunity." He's now willing to explore it further.

This is a common phenomenon, and it proves that the way you talk about your company can make all the difference. It works when you're trying to get your first customer as well. A potential customer will often have more interest in your product or service if they see you're talking to their competitors who might use you first and gain some advantage as a result.

You should never exaggerate or say something you can't back up. But I do want you to think more strategically. When you're approaching someone for business or money for your business, think about creating demand through competition.

Getting Down to Buzz-iness

I remember when I was building my first financial services company, a friend in Washington, D.C., said to me on the phone one day, "I'm hearing so much buzz about you."

What did she mean and how can "buzz" help you? Buzz can come in many forms but it's usually when people are talking about you, your ideas, or your products. This word-of-mouth advertising can really boost your business and even your own reputation.

How can you create buzz for your idea? As always, we start with our LifeNet. Let's say you've got an idea for a mobile pet store. You've noticed how kids in the neighborhood are always running for the ice cream truck. Why not have the same excitement when Pets-on-Wheels rolls up? You go to zones 2 and 3 of your LifeNet and discover all sorts of venues for your service. The elementary school would love to co-sponsor a local pet show. The nature center could also be a participant. You could check with your neighbor, the librarian, about posting flyers for the event. The list goes on.

Buzz can also be created by your choice of partners. Partners can include local companies carrying your product, companies helping you actually create the product, or companies using your product. When a partner or customer uses your product and they have a good experience, they'll talk about it. You can even work proactively to use them to help create buzz. For instance, you might ask a partner if they'd appear at a conference on your behalf and talk about the difference you made in their business.

Now, I know you're thinking, *Jennifer, I don't have the kind of contacts you do. How can I create buzz?* Look, I didn't have them either. When I was building my first company, I pursued people by making hundreds of cold calls. But I used what assets I did have and I ran on my passion. It made all the difference. I remember getting in to meet the president of Avon to talk about how my company could serve Avon reps. It's likely my very basic knowledge about women buyers proved valuable. The key is to simply put your best foot forward. What do you have in your bag of skills, knowledge, contacts, or positions that can somehow be of value to the person you want to meet? Believe me, if I can do it coming from nothing, you can, too.

QUICK TIP: Make People Demand You

Want to make people want you or your company's products or services? Here are some tips:

- Offer valuable advice. If you have an idea or insight, share it. This could be with a coworker or executive in your company, a business prospect, or an acquaintance.
- Build your profile. Make yourself an expert to the media. Meet with any local media that cover areas relating to your skills and knowledge. Be prepared to give insights into current trends or to offer specific tips.

• Focus on accomplishments. Talk about what's working, not what's not working with your venture or employer. Use language such as "Here's what we've done for other companies." Remember that people like being around other successful people.

Make People Demand You

We've talked a lot about creating demand for your product or service. Now I want to talk about creating demand for *you*! This is a little less tangible than creating demand for your product or service, but when people demand you, it means they value what you can offer, and it means more money, more recognition, and more opportunity for you.

Creating demand for you can also help make you more successful in your job. How many people do you see who keep getting job offers? Don't you wonder how they get them? They get them partly because they care for their LifeNet (we'll talk more about that in the next chapter) but also because they create demand for themselves. Creating demand for yourself can also help you build credibility to successfully start your own venture.

So how do you go about getting people to see you as the expert, the specialist, the one to hire or to fill that gaping void as a partner in a new venture?

My friend Kevin Miller is a great example. Kevin works for a large radio network selling advertising time. Kevin creates demand for himself in two ways.

First, he just has this personality that people want to be around. Don't underestimate the power of sheer likeability. Kevin is fun, engaging, and caring about the people he talks to. Remember, Sam Walton's likeability was a key factor in creating the company that now employs more people than any other company in the world.

Second, Kevin focuses on the customer's needs first, before his own. Rather than focusing on what he has in his suitcase to sell, he focuses on how he can help address the customer's needs or problems. He is able to put himself in the shoes of the company and think about ways they can better position or sell their product and affect their bottom line, sometimes by accessing his LifeNet. As a result, these customers want to listen to Kevin and his ideas. Kevin creates demand for himself and can win large clients, even when others cannot. This enables him to make more money and to position himself as very successful at what he does.

Finally, Kevin focuses on accomplishments. He talks about what's working, not what's not working. And remember, you don't have to be at the top of an organization or have a business at $50 million a year to have positive things to share that make others feel like you're a winner.

Create demand for yourself and people will seek you out. This can itself take you closer to the Zone—through a profitable consulting gig, a job offer with higher pay, or a request for you to join someone as a partner in a new venture.

The End Zone

We've talked about how you can go from an idea, like Erica Zohar's idea for creating attractive but comfortable clothes, to generating demand for your product or service. Erica Zohar became a millionaire in part because she used the tools at her disposal, coupled with her LifeNet, to test her idea first. How do you create demand?

- Test the market waters before diving in, by creating samples, using your LifeNet as a focus group, calling potential customers, and even turning to your former employer.
- Don't forget to accept feedback and make adjustments—they may be just the changes you need to propel you into the Millionaire Zone.
- Perceptions matter, so use *we* when discussing your plans, and avoid negative statements.

- You can generate ideas for in-demand products or services—just listen to the people around you (and do the exercise in this chapter!).
- Even if demand does not yet exist for your idea, that doesn't mean it's not a good idea! We've seen countless examples of that.
- Create demand for your product or service by creating competition, generating buzz, getting media attention, and making people demand you.

The more demand there is for you and your product, the better your chances of getting to the Millionaire Zone.

· 8 ·

Key 6: Getting by Giving

We've talked throughout this book about your LifeNet—that web of people, places, and resources that we must tap to get to a seven-figure fortune. It's made a big difference in my life and my success. I know it'll make a big difference in yours. Now let's talk about what you need to do to care for and nourish that LifeNet, so that it can continue to support you for a long time to come.

You can't just take without giving back. Well, let me rephrase that: You *can* just take without giving back, but your LifeNet won't be long for this world if you do. You'll find it an unnecessarily difficult and much longer journey to the Millionaire Zone, if you get there at all.

Your LifeNet plays such a vital role in your life—providing information, advice, introductions, and opportunities, along with emotional, financial, and practical support—it's like a living, breathing organism that requires care and feeding. Learning how to do this takes practice, but if you follow my suggestions, your LifeNet will grow as you grow and be there when you need it.

As you've no doubt guessed, I have found my LifeNet to be invaluable in helping me move further into the Millionaire Zone. But when I allow the people in my LifeNet to share in the wealth that they're helping me to create—whether that wealth sharing is financial or one of the myriad other ways to care for my LifeNet—that's when things really start to happen.

Giving back to your LifeNet means you'll be able to rely on that web of people, places, and resources for a long time to come, and you'll have a much easier time from the start getting your new venture off the ground.

This giving back can take various forms, and there are definitely some mistakes you want to avoid. First, let me tell you about my friend Bob Lorsch. He's exemplary at taking care of the vast numbers of people and places he counts in his LifeNet.

Bob's Story

Bob Lorsch was an inch away from dropping out of high school, but his mind was always ticking when it came to ways of making money. He did end up getting his diploma in summer school, but once he dove into the world of business he never looked back. He's gone from high school semidropout to one of the brains behind the original marketing launch of Microsoft's Windows. Once, a company asked him to create a business plan for them and then they rejected one of his ideas—a prepaid calling card concept marketed through retail stores (this was long before these things were ubiquitous in stores everywhere)—but he stuck to his idea and created a prepaid calling card program that he eventually sold, building his net worth to many tens of millions of dollars.

Today, because he is a master at selling himself, Bob has become a fixture in Los Angeles. He's often seen hanging out with the likes of Elton John, Gene Simmons, Diana Ross, Rod Stewart, and many other personalities on the business, entertainment, and political scene. He's a multimillionaire with a LifeNet that spans the globe. And no one knows how to leverage and take care of that resource like Bob Lorsch.

"I think one of the reasons that I have been successful is that in all my business endeavors, and as I go through my personal life, I look for ways to give. I look for ways to support people. I look for ways to inspire and motivate—and whether it's with money or with time, the more I put out, truly the more it seems that I get back," Bob says.

I remember seeing Bob in action at a fundraiser. Boy, does he know how to connect the dots. Bob serves on the Board of the Wildlife WayStation, which runs a sanctuary for tigers, lions, and other wild animals. Bob had attended an event for another non-profit, Best Friends, a dog and cat rescue organization. While at the Best Friends dinner, Bob had an idea: Why not offer Best Friends a dinner at the Wildlife WayStation (complete with tours and photos of tigers and other wild animals) as an auction item for Best Friends? The dinner was so popular as an auction item that Best Friends has auctioned off three WayStation dinners, raising nearly $30,000. Even though Bob works for a different charity, his efforts paid off for everyone. Best Friends raised more money and the WayStation was introduced to possible new givers. "Even four-legged creatures were helping four-legged creatures!" says Bob.

Sounds simple, right? But the beauty of what Bob did was that he connected two organizations that, until that night, had no connection. In doing so, he made invaluable contributions to both non-profits and put himself squarely in both of their LifeNets.

So, you might be saying to yourself, if he's getting no tangible benefit, why do it? But, you see, to Bob's way of thinking—the LifeNet way—the reward is immeasurable and invaluable.

"The more you give to the universe, the more you get back. That rule works for me daily," he says. In other words, he gives ideas, resources, support, and connections, and over time these gifts come back to him, with his well-cared-for LifeNet giving back to him in myriad ways.

"I view every situation and every single individual who comes into my life as important and someone who can affect my life in one of two ways: Either improve my net worth or improve my personal being because I know I've done something that's really changed their life," he says.

CHAPTER CHECK-IN: How Bob Gets by Giving

• Recognizes that every person he meets will impact his life in some way, not just financially
• Is always responsive, answering every e-mail and phone call or having someone do it on his behalf
• Introduces people in his LifeNet to each other, "connecting dots," so they can be successful
• Maintains information on everyone he meets to expand his LifeNet, and always has his own business card ready to give
• Finds ways to give back to causes he is passionate about through his business ventures

How Bob Reached the Millionaire Zone

• Set financial goals, starting when he was a salesman for smokeless cigarettes with a goal of making $100 a day; today his goal is to grow his current company to $1 billion in value
• Never censored his own ideas and, as a result, was hired repeatedly for his big ideas
• Turned a rejection for one idea—a prepaid calling card—into an opportunity he himself pursued
• Invested $5,000 of his own money, relied on credit cards, and went to friends and business contacts to raise additional funds
• Took the company public and grew his personal worth to tens of millions of dollars

---

Example from the Millionaire Zone
Oprah Winfrey, founder, Harpo Studios; host, *The Oprah Winfrey Show*

No. 235 on the Forbes 400
Net worth: $1.5 billion
Key strategy: Getting By Giving

It would be impossible in the limited space we have here to detail the ways in which Oprah Winfrey cares for and feeds her LifeNet. That task seems almost to be her mission in life. In fact, she's been quoted in *Success with an Open Heart: Oprah Winfrey* as saying, "My mission is to use this position, power, and money to create opportunities for other people."

Among the ways she's done this: Christmas gifts for 50,000 African children, extensive work for Habitat for Humanity, gifts for the studio audience of her television show, not to mention all the first-time authors who've been catapulted to stardom and the best-seller list thanks to her book club recommendations.

Back in 1988, she said she'd continue her TV show despite the amount of time and energy it takes, because "I've thought long and hard about the reality of doing four hundred more shows. I want to use television not only to entertain, but to help people lead better lives. I realize now, more than ever, that the show is the best way to accomplish these goals."

There's no doubt that, if you asked Oprah whether she could have gotten to where she is today on her own, without what I call her LifeNet, she'd say no. And that's why, every day, she gives back to those around her and those in need.

The Multiplier Effect

Isn't Bob's way of thinking compelling? He knows that every person he meets can change his life. Bob recognizes that his LifeNet is a living thing. Think of it as your personal tree of life. It starts out as a seedling. If you water, feed, and care for that seedling, it will grow into a sapling. The more you care for it, the more it will grow. It will grow so tall and strong that one day—if you keep caring for and feeding it—it will throw off seeds that will grow even more plants. That is the power of caring for and feeding your LifeNet.

As you care for your LifeNet, a wonderful thing will begin to happen. Opportunities to make money will come to you. I remember Bob telling me recently about a rare collection of sculptures to which he now has the exclusive rights to market and distribute. How did he get those rights? Well, sure, he has to be good at what he does—and he is. But it was his LifeNet—the people he had given to over the years—that put him in touch with the owners of the sculptures and now wanted Bob's expertise.

Desma, about whom we read in Chapter 3, is another great example. Do you recall the two opportunities that came to her? One was the resale shop; the other was Lady Valet. In both cases, people came to Desma with ideas and support for these businesses. They came to her because of her passion and the way she always unconditionally gives back to those around her.

And there's no question that as I have expanded my LifeNet and begun to care for it more than I did before, I've had more opportunities come my way. Friends from grade school and high school with whom I reconnected provide emotional and practical support— more than I had ever dreamed of—while the husband of one provides expertise related to my own real estate endeavors. In the last three months, four potential partner companies have reached out to my company. A few others have asked whether I would help them launch an exciting new business. Through yet another member of my LifeNet, I met an entrepreneur who manages a team of developers and excels at online marketing; he brings just the kind of energy, expertise, ethics, and support I may need for a possible new venture (stay tuned!).

When you treat your LifeNet like an important member of your family, like the living organism that it is, it will produce tangible results, including:

- When you nourish the people and organizations in your LifeNet, they will want to help you more. This is such a sim-

ple truth: If you treat people well, 9 times out of 10 they will be eager to treat you well in return.

• The more you make an effort to connect people and places and resources and information, the more people and places (or organizations) you will meet. One, two, or more of them might be the ticket in terms of helping you reach your goals. Call it the power of numbers.

• You will be in the mindset of helping others and seeking help from others, which is exactly the mindset you need to be in the Millionaire Zone! Remember, Zoners don't become that way by relying solely on themselves. They connect with others, they ask for help, they put their needs out into the world and, while they're waiting for help from others, they go on helping others.

• Humans are social creatures. We feel better when we help others. We're hard-wired to connect to one another. Too often we become disconnected. We spend all day chained to our desks and then spend all night at home in front of the TV. That existence is not well suited to vaulting you into the Zone. If you get out, call people, meet people, help people, take my word for it, you will feel better. And the better you feel, the more people will want to work with you.

• Finally, there's a ripple effect when you help others. We all have our own LifeNets. Taking care of your LifeNet will nourish other LifeNets.

So you can see there are some powerful benefits to treating your LifeNet with great care. But what are some ways to go about that? We'll turn to that next.

CHAPTER CHECK-IN: *Six Ways to Care for Your LifeNet*

In this section, we look at the ways you can care for your LifeNet:

• Give unconditionally.
• Make it routine.

- Track it.
- Connect the dots.
- Remember that little things make a difference.
- Reach out in tough times.

Give Unconditionally

Perhaps the most important thing when it comes to caring for your LifeNet is to give *unconditionally*. You've heard about the unconditional love of a parent for their child. You should operate the same way with your LifeNet. When you give of yourself without focusing on what you're getting back, your giving will be richer because it's authentic. You will be coming from a place of true care and concern.

Bev Khan, like Bob, knows what it means to give unconditionally. Bev was a schoolteacher who, after a divorce, "had to find a way to feed three kids or go on welfare." The most money she had ever earned as a schoolteacher was $7,500 a year, about 20 years earlier. On a dare from her former husband, she started what today is a $5 million business, placing technology professionals in high-paying jobs. And she started right at her kitchen table, by writing down the companies and people she knew in key positions, the people who could hire and fire.

"When I started, I formed the first group of people in the corporate world who I knew," says Bev. She started out placing bookkeepers and secretaries in jobs. She knew a friend of a friend who needed a job—and she found a job for that person. Her business took off from there, with that first successful client telling people he knew about Bev and her business. "My entire career has been about reaching out to people. And I've found that the smartest and most successful people will help you because they're secure in their knowledge." Those people helped Bev build her business.

Although Bev had to quit pursuing her MBA midstream because of the demands of work and family, she found the experience in-

strumental in growing her business. Through her business classes, she learned about marketing and expanded her business into that area, placing marketing professionals. They make more than bookkeepers—and that meant more revenue for Bev.

Now, she says, "I place people like chief technology or chief information officers. By giving them good, honest advice about their career, they end up in top positions. They want to give back to you," she says. "Nearly 90% of the business we have is repeat. If you help people succeed, their success then creates success for yourself."

How many millionaires have their own kitchen-table origins? It's a very common story among those in the Millionaire Zone.

Make Giving a Habit

Bev cares for her network daily by offering career advice. It's how she made a seven-figure fortune without having to spend money on advertising. Bob Lorsch practices caring for his LifeNet every day as well. Among other things, it helped him find new money-making opportunities and even new employees.

When it comes to caring for your LifeNet, you need to incorporate it into your everyday life, just like eating and sleeping. Don't approach it as a chore. View every person, entity, and resource as adding value to your venture and your life. Take time to tell them you care (in the ways I'll outline below).

This is a shift in mindset for many of us. In today's society, despite how small our world has become in this global economy, ironically we often feel isolated and cut off. We hunker down, keeping to ourselves even if we're not introverts, in part because of the stresses and demands of our daily lives.

It takes an effort to break the pattern of staying locked away in your Home Zone, using it as a crutch rather than as a springboard. But there are a few tricks to moving your life into a wider orbit. Like many of you, I find myself on airplanes. Before I was conscious of my LifeNet, I buried myself in my work, pounding away on my computer. Now I make it a point to stop, take a breath, and find out who's sitting next to me.

Here are some of the people I've met in the course of my travels:

- A bicycle shop owner from Aspen, Colorado, who shared with me his trick for paying bills on time, albeit the old-fashioned way. (The trick is to get your bills ready in an envelope, addressed and stamped. Scribble in the corner the date you need to mail them. Put them in order on the hall table, with those that need to be mailed first on top.)
- An original investor in Cisco who offered to introduce me to potential investors for my business
- A young couple: The husband worked at a prestigious investment firm and the wife attended law school and worked for a nonprofit; the wife took great interest in my work with American families and wanted to work with me.
- The head of a regional Young Presidents' Organization, who's since become a friend and assisted in reaching out to millionaires for this book

The list goes on.

Now I want you to open yourself up. The following exercise will help.

Exercise: Close your eyes. Take a few minutes to picture yourself in a setting with people all around you. It could be on an airplane, at work, or at a cocktail party. Think about how you typically interact with people. How do you see yourself? If someone talks to you, how do you react? Are you more of an extrovert or introvert?

Now envision yourself in the same situation, but this time open your mind to the possibilities. Picture the same person talking to you, only now consider what you might learn from this person, no matter who he or she is. Is it possible he can empower you with even just one piece of information?

Finally, think back on your life. What was the most stimulating conversation you've ever had with someone you hadn't known until then? What made the talk so inspiring? How did you feel? Do you remember any lessons learned or thoughts that stuck with you over the years? What would it be like to talk to that person again? What if I told you that it was possible to meet dozens of people like that person over the rest of your life, simply by growing your LifeNet? You can, and if you want to, you will!

Track Your LifeNet

You can't take care of your LifeNet if you don't know who's in it. You'll need some sort of basic system to track the people, places, and resources that comprise your LifeNet.

"My Rolodex has 9,600 names," Bob Lorsch says. "When I need something I can say, 'Who do I know in Grand Rapids?' And invariably there's someone I know in Grand Rapids. It's my world-wide network."

That's the power of keeping track of your LifeNet—being able to reach someone when you need to. Every time you meet someone, put their contact information in a database, plus a little bit about who they are and how you met.

"The fact is, building your network could be invaluable. I was in Vegas years ago and met someone and we shared a limo. I took his name and address, and nine years later I'm in a conference room buying his company," Bob says.

"I said to him, 'I know you, and I met you about nine years ago.' He said, 'No you don't.' I pulled him up on my database and said, 'Your wife is Marlene. You live in Chicago.' He thought I had hired someone to follow him!"

Just think about the power of the six degrees of separation. This is the notion that everyone in the world is separated by just six people from everyone else.

Bob's version is kind of a 72 degrees of separation. "There's a theory that if you make a list of the most important 72 people that you know in the world today, you can reach anybody in the world. I'm convinced of it."

Even if your database of contacts is small right now, over time it will grow. So get your database started. Put in all the people you know, from close family and friends to acquaintances. Everyone. Then think about the people they might know who could help you in your venture. You can start by reviewing the exercise in Chapter 3 where I helped you wire your LifeNet. Your best bet is to create a database on a computer so that you can back it up, take it with you, and send out communications effectively.

Every time you meet someone, record their name, the date you met, their address, e-mail, phone number, how you met, and any information on their personal life (married? kids? etc.). Also, record what type of work they do, and—this is the key—any challenges or needs they expressed. That way, should you meet someone in your LifeNet who can help that person, you'll remember to make that introduction.

The ideal database is probably a BlackBerry or Treo, but a database program like ACT! or Access is fine—even index cards are great, as long as the information is accessible and up to date. Or, you can do this at www.themillionairezone.com. This does not have to be some complex computer database. Just make sure you have the information easily accessible and that you back it up regularly.

Connect the Dots

Bob Lorsch's ability to step back and connect two people who were in his LifeNet but not yet in each other's is a great example of what I call connecting the dots. This might feel like it takes a lot of time to do, but it doesn't. In fact, the more you make caring for your LifeNet a priority, the more you will increase the members in your own LifeNet and enjoy the benefits in return.

I remember when my friend Cathi told me how she was searching for her next career move. It occurred to me that she would benefit by meeting my friend John, a former bank CEO. After all, Cathi used to work at a bank. And I figured John could benefit from her—he's got several businesses going and might be able to use a smart person with Cathi's experience. Today, several years later, they are friends who support each other in many ways, from Cathi getting a seat on a company's board of directors thanks to John's LifeNet, to John getting introductions to helpful people through Cathi.

If you stop and think about it, there are probably opportunities every day for you to connect dots. Step back and think of the people in your own LifeNet who can help the people or organizations you meet. The next time you meet someone, take the time to learn a bit about them. Then, do a mental run-through of all the people you know to see if you know someone who can help this new person. Be creative!

Remember, Little Things Make a Difference

I have a good friend, Stacy, who today is a powerful attorney in Los Angeles. We met when we were both on the board of a nonprofit that helps aging seniors find affordable housing. Because I had always been too busy, I finally decided to hit the pause button and reach out to her. We both had a similar get-it-done attitude, and I liked her professionalism. I thought she might make a great friend. Stacy was pregnant with her first child, so I decided I would make a small gesture and give her a teddy bear as a baby gift. Well, that little effort—which cost a whopping $10—went a long way. Stacy was so appreciative that not only did she embrace me as a friend but she has consistently introduced me to people and organizations in *her* LifeNet.

Here's the truth: You don't have to give a lot to make an impact. You don't even have to spend a lot of money. I certainly didn't. But think of it this way: To Stacy, the value of that small gesture was priceless regardless of the small investment of time and money it took me to give her that teddy bear.

Reach Out in Tough Times

Don't ever think you have nothing to offer. You have plenty to offer to the right person. The person who is helpful to someone in need is the person who will be remembered and rewarded. Those who are down today may well be riding high tomorrow. They may even be your boss one day.

Consider how Bob Lorsch approaches a simple jewelry purchase. "I was in New York recently and went to purchase something as a gift," he says. He treated the shopkeeper well, and exchanged business cards. "That person could become the next senior vice president of Tiffany or senator of New York. Who knows, they could end up working for me!"

Remember the aphorism that you should treat people well on your way up the corporate ladder, because one day you may encounter them again on your way down.

QUICK TIP: Six Mistakes to Avoid When Caring for Your LifeNet

This chapter talks about ways to *care* for your LifeNet and ways to *feed* your LifeNet. But here are six common mistakes people make in this process—mistakes that undermine the whole idea of supporting your LifeNet and of letting it support you.

- Don't assume someone isn't good enough. You never know where that person might end up one day—she could become your boss!
- Don't assume you'll never talk to this person again. It's a small enough world that you could meet again, or you could meet someone this person knows. There's no point in leaving anything except a good impression.
- Don't judge a book by its cover. Some of the wealthiest, most

powerful people in the world are unassuming. Treat everyone as worthy.

- Don't think you don't have time to properly thank someone. It doesn't take long to reward them for helping you. The truth is, you can't afford *not* to take the time.
- Don't think you don't need to repay someone. If you don't give back to your LifeNet, it will stop giving to you. Those in the Zone consider this a key part of business.
- Don't discount someone because they can't offer exactly what you're looking for. They might have other valuable skills, experiences, or resources that *will* help you.

CHAPTER CHECK-IN: *The Two Primary Ways to Feed Your LifeNet*

- Provide nonfinancial help, such as expertise, connections, or support.
- Offer financial rewards.

Feed with Expertise, Connections, Support

So now you know how to care for your LifeNet. The next step is to think about how you can really nourish your LifeNet. What are some specific ways you can give back when a member of your LifeNet has helped you?

Let's use Jake as an example. Jake has a passion for fixing cars, and wants to start an auto-body repair shop. A friend of Jake's, Mark, sets Jake up with one of the car rental companies in the neighborhood so he can get their business to repair any rental cars that have been in an accident. That one introduction could set Jake well on his way to the Millionaire Zone. How could Jake reward Mark for the referral? Jake could do what some people (but not enough) do: Write a thank-you note. Will that encourage Mark to take time out of his busy schedule help him again? Probably not. In fact, Mark might even be a little ticked off that he didn't get more commensurate recognition. Jake could take Mark and his wife out to an expensive restaurant. Okay, that's sounding a little better.

But what else could Jake do? Well, I suppose Jake could give Mark and his wife plane tickets to their favorite resort, which might equal roughly one or two of the sales orders Jake received through his new business relationship with the car rental company.

Not bad, but let's think big picture. Jake can keep his eyes and ears open to help Mark in his own job or venture. Maybe Mark has dreams of starting up his own luxury classic car rental company. Jake might be able to provide his own expertise on which types of vehicles are most reliable, or most popular. Jake can be alert to finding someone in his LifeNet who can help Mark. The giving back of our personal time, knowledge, and skills can be the best pay-back because the benefits are so much longer-lasting than a dinner or vacation.

Of course, how you give depends on the situation. You can give back on a very simple scale, as demonstrated by Erica Zohar, the clothing maker. She turns to her LifeNet every time she designs a new line of clothes. She asks friends what they think of her styles. They give her their honest critique. In return, she lets them take some clothes home. Do you think her friends would be helpful to her again? You bet.

And don't forget that you can also volunteer or contribute to someone's charity. Someone who's already achieved financial success may appreciate more your support of a cause that is close to their heart and allows them to leave a legacy.

Show Them the Money

Sometimes it makes the most sense to reward people in your LifeNet financially. Who doesn't want to make money by helping *you* make money on your way to the Zone?

It is not uncommon, for example, if someone helps you make a sale to offer them a piece of the pie. Let me give you an example of someone I know personally. Larry Campbell came across an opportunity to take a new computer-security software program to a variety of industries. One of those was the government sector. Larry sat down with his friend Frank, who was familiar with government agencies.

Larry had already struck his deal with the company that owned the software. Rather than working as an employee getting a paycheck, Larry gets 15% of product revenue as long as his customers pay for the product. To give you an idea on the numbers, if Larry makes one sale to a government body with 20,000 users, his share of the $2 million in gross sales would be $300,000—each year! He'd be a Zoner in about three years on one sale alone.

Now Larry understands the power of money. He knows he can't go after all those prospects himself; he'd never find the time for his other ventures or his family. So Larry decided to compensate Frank 7.5%, half of his 15% share for any introductions that lead to a successful sale. Do you think Frank is going to be motivated to act, and act fast?

There are many ways to fairly and appropriately structure compensation for someone who helps build your wealth. But a word of caution. I am not advocating anything that presents a conflict of interest. In Larry's case, it would obviously be a conflict if Frank was an employee or even a consultant of any government agency for which he was also soliciting business. So please keep this in mind as you move forward.

QUICK TIP: How to Create a Win-Win Partnership

Whether on the job or in your own venture, you want to be able to structure relationships that will take your project to the next level. Here are the three key questions to ask:

- What do they want? Ask yourself what would make your prospective partner more successful. It might be revenue, new customers, or even new ideas.

- What can I give? Look to yourself, your business, or your employer to see what you can give back. Make certain you can deliver, otherwise it will inevitably hurt your credibility and the relationship.
- What instills long-term commitment? Relationships are often formed with the best intentions but fall apart because there is no incentive for one party to continue. This is one reason compensating a partner on an ongoing basis can often be the most beneficial.

Managing Your Care and Feeding Time

How do you find the time to devote to your LifeNet, let alone your new venture? No doubt about it, life is busy. Even before trying to turn our passion into profits, we're all swamped with trying to support ourselves and our families.

But it's not as hard as you think as long as you're organized. If you follow the tips I offer here for managing your time, you'll find you can care for and feed your LifeNet. By achieving that, you'll find your LifeNet partners will be pitching in with your venture, saving you valuable time and energy.

CHAPTER CHECK-IN: How to Manage
Your Care and Feeding Time

In the next section, we look at how to organize your time for care and feeding.

- Do it now.
- Check e-mail early and often.
- Keep appointments.
- Structure your meetings.

Do It Now

When you're around serious entrepreneurs, you'll notice a get-it-done mentality. There's a sense of urgency to everything they do. Adopt that attitude and you're halfway to the Millionaire Zone.

Instead of thinking *Oh, I really should get back to Sheila to thank her for that lead*, do it right then and there. Or choose a time or times in the day to handle your return calls and e-mails. Care and feeding of your LifeNet does not require a huge investment of time or money. Think about how that teddy bear I bought my friend really touched her, and led to her keeping me in her LifeNet for years to come.

E-mail Early and Often

Since e-mail is now the common mode of communication, be sure to use it regularly. If you're not on e-mail, get on it. For the $15 per month or so, it is an investment that will allow you to manage your time and access the latest management tools. Responding to people in a timely fashion encourages the same from others. It will also keep stuff from piling up in your inbox.

Keep Appointments

I'll never forget my boss-to-be, when I worked in the State Treasurer's Office, chastising me after I rescheduled a lunch with him. He pointed out that canceling meetings lowers your credibility since you didn't do what you said you would do. I felt horrible about it because I knew he was right. It was a lesson that has always stuck with me.

When people take time for you, you need to respect and appreciate that time. To cancel or reschedule means you are not only failing to respect their time, you are also now taking up more of their time to accommodate you because you both have to reschedule.

While we're on the subject, let me address my favorite pet peeve: people who are late for meetings. Now, unfortunately, we are all guilty of this at one time or another. I have gotten much better myself, but used to always try to cram too much into my schedule, always running behind.

A banker friend of mine tells a good story. "When I was a young trainee at the bank, I kept a vice president waiting as we were headed to a client lunch. He was an older gentleman, a trust officer who had been with the bank for over 40 years and was nearing retirement. His customers loved and respected him. But he looked stern as I finally met him at the elevator. 'Ross,' he said to me, 'I only have one virtue: I'm punctual.'"

I believe that chronic tardiness is a subtle kind of snobbery. It tells people "I can keep you waiting because I'm more important than you are." Don't let that be you.

Structure Your Meetings

Never go into a meeting, or even make a phone call, without knowing exactly what you're going to discuss and what your desired outcome is. Be clear and focused. Have a written agenda. Ask the person how much time they have and pace yourself accordingly. Be sure to allow for time at the end to ask them how you can contribute to their LifeNet.

The End Zone

This chapter is all about the care and feeding of your LifeNet. Here's why it's so important:

- Those whom you nourish will want to help you succeed.
- You will be in the habit of helping others and of seeking help from them. This is key to successfully reaching the Millionaire Zone.

- Helping out your LifeNet will prompt people to remember you and to value you. This will lead to more opportunities for you, whether you hope to move higher in your career or start your own venture.

Here's a summary of how best to care for and feed your LifeNet:

- Give without expecting anything back. Often your interactions with others won't lead to an immediate benefit back to you. Just be patient—you'll see that caring for and feeding your LifeNet will come back you in many ways, at another point in time.
- Make the care and feeding of your LifeNet a daily habit. You never know who you'll meet or how they might help you at some point in the future.
- Keep track of your LifeNet—who they are, how to reach them, what their needs are—so that you can always give help and ask for help right when you need it.
- Connect people in your LifeNet to each other.
- Remember that even one helpful phone call can go a very long way in the care and feeding of your LifeNet.
- Reach out to people no matter what their current financial situation. You never know where they'll end up working tomorrow, or ten years down the road.
- Remember: The two key ways to feed your LifeNet involve financial support and nonfinancial support, such as your expertise, connections to others, or emotional support.

I want to leave you with one final story that shows how easy it is to put these steps into action, and how much impact you can have on someone's life when you follow these practices.

I recently ran into a fellow member of my gym whom I hadn't seen in a while. She thanked me profusely for my help. At first, I couldn't remember to what she was referring. As she spoke, I recalled she had been looking for advice on how to change her career.

She had been looking for work in her specialty, which was public relations. That's a very clubby competitive world. I remember encouraging her to broaden her search beyond PR firms to companies that might need corporate communications help. Armed with that advice, and with a partner she found by tapping into her LifeNet, she started a nonprofit that assists public companies in dealing with shareholder issues. Her company had only been up and running for a few months, but she was extremely pleased with her progress.

I was reminded once again that one good deed, no matter how seemingly inconsequential—I hadn't even remembered this one!—can resonate so positively in your LifeNet.

With the proper care and feeding, your LifeNet team will help you in ways you never dreamed possible on your way to the Millionaire Zone.

· 9 ·

Key 7: Turn Rejection into Opportunity

We are by nature creatures who strive for a sense of self-worth. When we're told "Don't do that" or "That's a lousy idea," we take it personally. We may realize only later that the comment was based on specific issues related to our product or service, not to us.

Still, because we've tied ourselves so closely to our venture or our career, it's tough not to feel that any rejection of our work is also a rejection of us. The big problem is, because we fear that pain, we often put ourselves in situations to avoid even the possibility of rejection. The result? We avoid risk.

Now, I know the pain of rejection, believe me. I can give you countless examples, and you'll read a few here. It feels like a punch in the stomach. But what I discovered during my research for this book—and in my many conversations with people who've already reached the Millionaire Zone—is that we are not alone. Many of them failed in their first, second, or even third ventures: the ultimate form of rejection.

I'm not pretending that mastering our feelings about rejection is easy. According to one study by doctors at UCLA, we respond to rejection just as we do to physical pain. That is, two parts of the brain seem to respond to the pain of rejection in the same way as physical pain.

"While everyone accepts that physical pain is real, people are tempted to think that social pain is just in their heads," said Matthew Lieberman, one of the paper's three authors and an assistant professor of psychology at UCLA, according to an article in *Science*. "But physical and social pain may be more similar than we realized."

The theory is that the pain of being rejected may have evolved because social bonds are so important for most mammals' survival. "Going back 50,000 years, social distance from a group could lead to death and it still does for most infant mammals," Lieberman said. "We may have evolved a sensitivity to anything that would indicate that we're being excluded. This automatic alarm may be a signal for us to reestablish social bonds before harm befalls us."

Taking this a step further, psychologist Mark Leary posited in a ground-breaking new theory that self-esteem is *not* something we bolster from within. He says self-esteem is a reflection of our relationships (think LifeNet!). Individualism doesn't heighten our self-esteem, but strong relationships with others can. Plus, Leary says, we're hard-wired to detect the signs that someone doesn't like or approve of what we're doing. That's further evidence of how paramount our LifeNet is as an ongoing affirmation of what we're doing. Don't assume you can sustain your positive attitude by yourself.

In conversations and in my own experiences, I've learned ways of dealing with rejection. And you can do it, too. You can convert rejection into opportunities to learn, to move your venture or your career forward, and to get closer to the Zone. This chapter gives you tips for coping with rejection, plus exercises to improve your chances of success in the face of rejection.

Now let me tell you about my friend Kevin, who took more rejection punches than you can imagine.

Kevin's Story

Kevin DiCerbo faced plenty of obstacles while he was trying to get his skin-care business, Celibre, off the ground. They were the kind of hurdles that would've stopped most people. In fact, if I were to back up a bit and tell you that Celibre was Kevin's third attempt at building a seven-figure fortune, you would have thought he was downright crazy. But Kevin understood that rejection is just part of the game. This time, though, the rejection was almost unbearable.

"The biggest rejection I faced was getting financing. I was working nights and weekends on this concept and was putting any extra money away for the business. But I still needed a loan. I figured I needed $100,000," Kevin said.

Kevin wanted a bank loan rather than getting funds from an investor, so that he wouldn't have to give up ownership in the business. "But to get a small business loan, you have to own a home or other property. I had neither."

So he spent a lot of time looking for funding. "I went to at least 20 different banks for SBA loans and got turned away at each one," he says. But he never let those rejections happen without tapping into the possible opportunity each presented. And he turned to his college network and asked them what he should do.

"I kept meeting with people to say, 'Okay, so you're telling me you can't do it, but do you know someone who could provide me with a loan?' I met with about 50 people for financing or to ask for referrals. The first bank said they couldn't do it but they said go visit these three banks. They all said no and then they'd refer me to three more."

Finally, Kevin says, "I found *one* out of those 50 people who believed in me and my business. They wanted to increase their portfolio even if this loan didn't have real estate attached to it."

Kevin did eventually succeed. The key is he didn't let the rejection get to him. "It was a roller coaster. One day you think you have a hot lead and the next day it completely dries up. You think you have a lease location for the first storefront but then they want a personal guarantee from someone with a net worth of $1 million. So I felt dejected a lot. But if you believe in the idea, you have to keep moving forward."

CHAPTER CHECK-IN: How Kevin Turned Rejection into Opportunity

- When turned down for a loan, always asked for a referral to another bank rather than leaving empty-handed
- Decided in advance how he wanted to structure a partnership with a doctor rather than finding a doctor and then structuring a deal
- Used his LifeNet successfully to locate the right doctor-partner for his skin-care business, one willing to work within his financial limits
- Remained flexible, structuring a relationship that gives the doctor some cash each month plus a share of the business
- Never, ever gave up and never took a rejection personally

How Kevin Reached the Millionaire Zone

- Before starting Celibre, tried two ventures through which, despite making little to no money, he developed contacts and experience and confirmed his entrepreneurial drive
- Reached out to doctors and nurses through his LifeNet, took them to lunch, and increased his knowledge of the skin-care industry
- Believed in his concept for Celibre so much, thanks to his considerable research, that he chose to risk his own money and consequently maintained majority ownership in the company, now worth $5 million
- Viewed himself as a better investment than his home; chose to rent at $2,000 a month instead of buying a home (with a $4,000 monthly payment for the same size as his rental) so

that he could put money aside to be a down payment for the business. As Kevin said, "I believe I can get a better return by investing in myself."

- Delays gratification: "I invest rather than consume. I don't buy new cars, clothes, or other toys. I'll be a bigger consumer later, but not when I can't afford to be."

Example from the Millionaire Zone
Steven Jobs, cofounder and CEO, Apple Computer
No. 67 on Forbes 400
Net worth: $3.3 billion
Key strategy: Turn Rejection into Opportunity

Steve Jobs knows rejection. We all know that as cofounder with Steve Wozniak of the iconic Apple Computer company, Jobs was instrumental in bringing personal computing into our homes. But despite his creating the famous Apple II computer and, later, the Macintosh, in the mid-1980s, disputes over the direction the company was taking caused the board of directors to strip Jobs of his duties at the very company he had created. Talk about rejection!

So what did he do? Did he give up, call it quits, decide he just wasn't cut out for running a company? Not exactly. Jobs went on to found another computer company, NeXT Computer. A few years later, Apple Computer bought NeXT. Because Jobs continued to focus on developing great computer operating systems and software, rather than giving up after being rejected, he ended up back at the company he'd founded, eventually regaining his place at the helm, and the title of chief executive officer.

Ever since, he's brought even more accolades and profits to the company, not to mention technological innovation combined with sleek design to consumers worldwide. Just take a look around as you walk down the street: All those white ear-buds connected to iPods confirm that claim.

If any of us who have trouble handling rejection could take just one inch of Jobs' drive and commitment to success—his unwilling-ness to let rejection stop him in his tracks—we'd be in the Million-aire Zone in no time.

The Waiting Game

Kevin's story shows, if anything, the value of never taking no for an answer. It also demonstrates the payoff of waiting for the right per-son to come along. But how do you remain persistent, in the face of rejection over a long period of time? That's when your passion kicks in. Kevin's passion for the skin-care business emerged after he went through a harrowing experience trying to get a birthmark re-moved. Someone claiming to be a doctor really botched the job. But that ultimately drove Kevin to make sure others wouldn't go through the same experience. That passion is why he can handle rejection. His business is a core value of his life, and he won't let a lack of money stop him.

Critical to Kevin's mission is to make sure people can find help with birthmarks and other skin-care issues, like protruding veins, acne, and wrinkles. So, in order for his business to work, he needed to find a medical doctor to oversee the treatments. Using his LifeNet, Kevin sent out an e-mail to his college friends, asking them if they knew any physicians with entrepreneurial spirits.

Kevin eventually talked to ten different doctors. Nine of them wanted more money than he was willing to pay. "I had doctors tell me, 'I'll do it for $10,000 per month,'" Kevin says. "Yikes! That's a lot!"

For some people in Kevin's situation, those responses might have felt like rejection. Some might have given up on the idea alto-gether. Not Kevin.

"I had that birthmark removed, and it was horrible. The way that guy had his business set up. I'd never do that. I saw a need for this service," he says. Eventually, Kevin met Dr. Kaplan through a friend of his. When they talked about working together, they shared similar ideas of how the business arrangement would work. "The numbers we talked about were pretty close. He receives some fee plus he owns part of the business," Kevin says.

Once again, Kevin's passion for the business helped him see past those who essentially rejected him with unmanageable demands.

What Rejection?

Rejection can come in many forms. For Kevin, it was the rejection not of his idea—but of his financial qualifications. He didn't have the credit for the banks and he didn't have the cash to pay a doctor. Having the right financial backing is a huge issue, which we'll get to in the next chapter where I go into how to fund your venture.

Rejection doesn't even have to involve people. Any failure feels like rejection. How many people do you know who pulled entirely out of the stock market after the tech-boom crash in 2000? Ironically, investors who bought stocks after the market plummeted since then have shown good returns to date. They turned rejection into opportunity.

But market or personal crashes don't have to signal the end of your dreams. Turning a no into a yes, turning rejection into acceptance, turning failure into success—these are characteristics of great achievers. They do not take rejection personally.

Sure, you might be thinking, *That's easy for you to say, but that's just not the way I handle things.* Don't worry. There are ways to turn that thinking around. But first, let's look at some people who are pros at handling rejection.

CHAPTER CHECK-IN: How the Fear of Rejection Hampers You

- You take a *no* as a reflection of your personal worth.
- You censor your ideas.

- You don't act confident, believable, or passionate.
- You don't feel in control.

Just a Part of Business

Depending on the work experience you have, you might not realize that overcoming repeated rejection is a fundamental part of business. Salespeople face more rejection than anyone else. That's why most sales managers train and prepare their salespeople to learn how to overcome objections. They expect to make 100 calls because it takes that many to get 35 meetings and the 35 meetings will result in only three actual sales. That's a 97% failure rate. Talk about rejection!

No matter what you're selling, there will be some people who won't buy it. Yet hundreds of thousands of businesses, run by everyday people like you and me, succeed because they understand that it's a numbers game. If you keep at it, you'll pile up enough wins to be a winner.

There's a well-known saying among salespeople: "A no is just a yes deferred." Any time you try to accomplish anything of value in your life, especially involving change, someone will say no. Change is threatening. It involves a shift in our Comfort Zones. If I ask you to try a different breakfast cereal, I'm going out of my Comfort Zone by risking rejection and you're going out of your Comfort Zone by considering a change from your favorite brand. You may say no initially, but if I tell you it's the best cereal I've ever tasted, plus it's low in fat and calories, you may try it. If you like it, we will have both successfully expanded our Comfort Zones.

Now, some of us tend to give up in the face of rejection more easily than others, but I can help you persist in the face of rejection. Let me show you the first step.

Don't Censor Yourself

Have you ever been in a business meeting, a class lecture, or simply with a group of acquaintances? A good idea pops into your head, you start to say something, but then you check yourself and don't say it? I'll admit I have. I've been afraid my idea would sound stupid, which is strange because in school I'd raise my hand every chance I'd get! But censoring yourself is a form of self-rejection. You will never reach the Millionaire Zone if you censor your own thoughts and ideas. Let me share a story.

Bob Lorsch barely finished high school. Now he's a multimillionaire. One of the reasons for his success has to do with how he handled one no!

When he was in his late forties, Bob was asked to develop a new business program for a phone company. After much research, he came back with a plan that included, among other things, an idea for a prepaid calling card—long before they were popular.

The company rejected Bob's suggestion. Bob refused to give up. He asked whether he could execute the idea himself. With just $5,000 of his own money, some credit-card debt, and investments from friends, he turned his idea into a company that at one time had a market value in excess of $1 billion, which he later sold to AT&T.

"I could have thought *Gee, my client didn't think it was a good idea, so it must not be,*" Bob says now. "By not censoring myself, and believing in my idea, I went out and hit the cover off the ball and created wealth for me and a lot of people."

Bob says the fact that he never censors his ideas is one secret to his success. Sure, he says things that someone may not agree with. He may even get laughed at. But what do people remember about Bob? His great ideas.

"Many people come up with great ideas but they are too intimidated by their surroundings to share those ideas, so they censor themselves," Bob explains. "Don't be your own worst enemy."

QUICK TIP: Three Powerful Ways to Turn No into Yes

- A LifeNet Referral: There's nothing like the power of being able to say, "John Doe suggested I talk to you." People are much more receptive to your message if they know you've come to them through a friend, family member, or other member of their own LifeNet. You can use that referral in letters, e-mails, and in-person meetings.
- A LifeNet Requestor: An even better strategy is to find the right member of your LifeNet to initiate the introduction on your behalf. Say you want to meet a vice president of marketing. You discover through your LifeNet that the sister of a former colleague knows that person well. If she will contact the VP with a message along the lines of "Here's someone you should meet," he or she will be even more receptive to your message.
- Yes Conditioning: Let's say there's a good chance someone will turn down your idea or request. How can you increase the odds they'll say *yes*? By conditioning them—that is, getting them into the habit of saying *yes*! Here's how it works: You condition them to say *yes* by getting them to say *yes* repeatedly. How do you do that? By asking them questions to which they are very likely to respond *yes*. Once you've conditioned them this way, they're more inclined to say *yes* —even to something to which they otherwise might have said no. To get those initial *yeses*, ask for something that brings a benefit to them. Example: "Fred, I'm holding a conference in the city and I could give you some free advertising by posting your company logo in the brochure—just my way of saying thanks. Are you interested in that?" Fred, of course, says *yes*. He begins to associate your questions with positive things. Now, the next time you ask for something, Fred will be more inclined to answer with a *yes*.

CHAPTER CHECK-IN: Opportunities in Rejection

In this section of the chapter, we talk about the opportunities that exist every time you get rejected:

* New leads for more business
* Advice on what you did wrong, and suggestions on where to go in the future
* More time to look for the *right* situation
* A kick in the pants, when rejection spurs you on to do better

Getting New Leads for More Business

One big opportunity you'll always find embedded in rejection: new leads. We talked about how Kevin kept getting more bank loan referrals with each rejection. I remember when a company I wanted to partner with couldn't work us into their organization as fast as I wanted. But a few months later, the CEO called and said, "Jennifer, I just met with a company you have to talk to. They're trying to help large Fortune 500 companies offer financial advice to their employees and they need an unbiased solution like yours." That initial rejection led to a referral that really helped my business along.

The beauty of the LifeNet is that, with all the support you receive and all the connections you make, there are always other resources out there when you need them. If you deal with rejection with the right attitude, you can often impress the very people who put roadblocks in your path. They may even lead you to other resources, as they did for Kevin. Get those leads, and keep building your LifeNet.

Source of Advice or Information

Even if a company has rejected you or your product or service, ask about that company's target customer and their needs. Has it done any surveys? Does it get complaints from customers? How is the current economy affecting it? If you're building an advisory board, perhaps the person you're meeting with would make a good addition.

Once I went to a large nonprofit to talk about helping retirees. The nonprofit wasn't the right match for my services, but it had been thinking about what I had to offer. Because rejection was a non-issue, I was able to gather some important information, such as how frequently retirees wanted to access advice, who wanted online advice and who didn't, and how the current economy was making my service more valuable than ever to retirees.

A Kick in the Pants

Sometimes, a rejection can give you just the kick in the pants you need to get to the Millionaire Zone. Cecelia McCloy shared this story with me as I was writing this book.

"I had been unhappy with my corporate position for more than a year," she told me. "Finally, I flew halfway across the country to meet my supervisor for dinner, as he was on the East Coast and I was on the West Coast. At dinner, he told me he was reorganizing, and that he was moving my department under someone else! I was furious and quit right at dinner and stormed out of the restaurant. Back at the hotel, I realized what I had done! I turned my back on a big salary, lots of stock options. I called my husband, and he asked me what I was going to do. I told him that everyone else in California was an entrepreneur and what was wrong with us doing that? We're just as smart as everyone else. So we started our science and engineering business and today we have revenues of $8 million. It's amazing what getting angry will do for motivation!"

Think about it: Cecelia felt rejected by her boss's action, and she got angry. She could have swallowed her pride and gone along with the reorganization. Or, she could have moped along for months, stuck in feelings of injustice and unfairness. Instead, Cecelia used the situation as motivation to propel herself into the Zone.

Winning Even When You're Rejected

By now you can see that, even though it might seem counterintuitive, there are many benefits to be derived from rejection.

Here's a personal story. I remember when I was about to graduate from college. I was working for the Los Angeles city controller while attending school full-time, and I was thinking about getting my first job after graduation. After some initial interviews, I got an offer to become the deputy press secretary to the Los Angeles mayor. I was pretty excited. It was a job that would put me in the middle of all sorts of interesting issues—from trade and commerce to affordable housing. Then I got a call from the press secretary; she told me that in fact I didn't get the job because the mayor wanted to hire someone with more experience working in government. I was disappointed—that rejection hurt!—but I understood, so I kept looking.

About two months later I got a call from the wife of the deputy mayor at the time. She had a lead. "Kathleen Brown is running for state treasurer and she needs a press secretary—someone who has some experience but who won't cost an arm and a leg," she told me. That was quite an opportunity. I could really grow my skills and knowledge and, if she were elected, I'd be moving up to the state capitol. But getting the job was still a long shot in my mind. I was afraid of rejection and I didn't really think I'd get it because, at 23, I had very little experience. I went through the interview, feeling a bit like a dope, and thinking *There is just no way this is going to happen.* Afterward, I got a call from her adviser. "Well, you're a little green," he said, "but we'd like to hire you." Wow!

Can you see how when we're rejected—as I was in the mayor's office—that it's often because something better is waiting for us around the corner? I'm such a big believer in that because I've seen it happen so many times in my life and to so many people I know. And I can tell you that if I had gotten that job in the mayor's office, I would have been so over my head, it probably would have ended badly and I would have lost all enthusiasm for government service. I may not have taken the path that led me to writing this book and sharing stories about how I and others got to the Millionaire Zone.

Leaving Your Job the Right Way

Now Cecelia—who quit in a rage and then started her own company—did make something out of that initial rejection, but she might have burned fewer bridges if she'd gone back to make amends with her boss. There's no doubt that losing a job is tough, and you're probably mad as hell at everyone around you. But because you're likely to run into these people again, your goal should be to leave in as positive a way as possible. Whether you're leaving because you chose to or not, consider these people as part of your LifeNet.

When you leave, make sure you create new opportunities for yourself. Request that:

- Senior management will serve as a reference.
- The company will consider working with you in any venture you initiate.
- You are kept in mind for future job positions.

Consider these other strategies to create goodwill and new opportunities:

Be supportive of your colleagues while you're still on the job. Wayne Finkel, the auditor who now runs his own successful auditing firm, handled the subcontractors with whom he worked with care and respect. When he critiqued their work, he did it face-to-face, always highlighting the positive. Now some of those 40 auditors routinely throw business his way.

Give more than the standard two weeks' notice. Wayne gave two months' notice rather than two weeks because he wanted to maintain good relationships with his employer—who then funneled work to his new company.

Inform your peers. Tell as many people as possible—colleagues and others—why you're leaving. Spend time with those who might be able to assist you in any of the ways we've talked about. Chances are, you can use your LifeNet to help them and they can use theirs to help you.

Share ideas. After you leave, consider occasionally e-mailing an idea or sending an article to people at your former employer. This keeps you top of mind and builds the relationship because you're someone who's thinking about them. In general, keep in touch with former colleagues and supervisors.

CHAPTER CHECK-IN: Reduce the Chance of Rejection

Sure, rejection offers opportunities, but it's still best to avoid it if possible. In this section, we discuss:

- Do your due diligence.
- Listen first.
- Admit to problems up front.

Reduce the Chance of Being Rejected

There are benefits to rejection. But that doesn't mean we want to rush out and encourage it! Here are some ways to minimize rejection.

Do your due diligence. If you're meeting with someone, make sure they're the *right* person. Always make sure you've done your homework. You would never go on a job interview without knowing a thing or two (or ten!) about the company. Learn all you can.

Listen first. Don't go in blabbing away about yourself right away. Even if you've studied the situation beforehand, *listen* first. Then ask questions so that you know precisely how to meet your customer's needs.

This is often referred to in sales lingo as "consultative selling." After selling my first company, I met with the CEO of a major financial institution. I prepared three ideas for his business, summarized on a sheet of paper. What an impact! The power of listening to their needs and then offering customized solutions not only minimized rejection—it built up credibility in their eyes.

Admit to problems up front. If someone you're meeting with identifies a problem or criticizes you, don't be defensive. Acknowledge their concerns and tell them the steps you're prepared to take to fix the problem. Once the situation has been resolved, let them know immediately. Your credibility will be restored and they will be more confident about working with you again.

Try These Exercises

Here are some exercises to help you control your reaction to rejection.

This first one is aimed at getting a little deeper at how rejection feels and how you react to it. The more we understand our reactions to events, the better we get at controlling those reactions.

Exercise: Think of a time you were rejected. Maybe you didn't get a job or a promotion, or you asked someone to go on a date. Write down three words to describe how you felt at the exact moment you were rejected.

Now, write down the longer-term impact that rejection had on you. In what way did that rejection affect your life?

Take a look at the difference between your worst fears and feelings and the actual reality. I bet, if I could read what you wrote, that nothing really terrible ever came from the time when you were rejected. In fact, for most people, their life went down a better track, and something better came along.

Now, here's an exercise to help you learn to manage how you react to rejection, turning it into something that we manage, rather than something that controls us.

Exercise: Try asking someone for something small that you're pretty sure will be rejected. Examples might be returning a used article of clothing for a cash refund or asking your bank for free checking. How does it feel? Probably, because it was something small and you were prepared for a no, you feel more in control. Not bad. Now, ask someone for something a little bigger. Again, you're in control. You're prepared for a no. Now, that wasn't so bad, was it? You're still intact, still alive. You have your health, your family, and much more. Now you're ready to begin responding creatively to a no.

Exercise: Write down past scenarios in which you've succeeded. Think through them and write down the skills and knowledge it took to achieve that success. In other words, keep a success journal. Write in it often. Refer to it often, especially after you've experienced rejection.

Exercise: Create a kudos file. Write down what other people said about you when you achieved some success. Record all the exact words of praise they offered. And, keep copies of e-mails and letters from people in which they offer praise.

It's All about Control

The reason we often take rejection badly is because we are allowing others to have control over our feelings. What if, instead, you take back control? Instead of feeling hurt and rushing away to have a pity party, hold an imaginary conversation with this person. Say, "Thank you for letting me know that this is not the right opportunity. I am now free to go find the right opportunity." Isn't that liberating? Going with the flow, rather than fighting it. Remember that saying "When a door closes, a window opens somewhere else!"

Tips for Coping with and Learning from Rejection

Successful people—in sales especially—know rejection is part of the game, so they simply put it to work for them by following some rules. Adopt the following six practices in your everyday life and you'll find rejection isn't the problem you thought it was.

See the big picture. Good salespeople know this is short-term pain that will diminish as they keep their eye on the big picture. This short-term pain is simply part of the longer process of success and achieving what you want. You never know where the next opportunity will come from.

Wayne Finkel, who quit corporate America to start his own auditing company, faces rejection every time he tries to get a new company to accept his services. But he doesn't take their hesitancy and distrust personally.

"We get rejected all the time," Wayne says. For instance, he says, "I'm trying to get into a particular foreign bank. At this point I can't seem to get in with him. He said he was going to meet with me but he hasn't called me back. I don't want to hassle him, but I will give him a couple of courtesy calls. At some point, he'll get too much work and he'll call me. I do feel a little rejected because I haven't won his business yet, but I'm still in his testing zone where he doesn't know and trust me yet."

Take chances. You need to take some chances in order to be successful. This is what we talked about in Chapter 4, about shifting your Comfort Zone. The key is to remember that you have your LifeNet as a safety net. If you're not making mistakes in the process of reaching the Millionaire Zone, then you're staying in your old Comfort Zone and not doing what you need to do to build your wealth.

The End Zone

With rejection comes opportunity! Consider these benefits of rejection.

- If you're rejected, ask why—and then use the answer to improve your product or service, so you can better serve the next person.
- Get a referral to someone else who might be better served by you, your product, or your service.
- Despite the rejection, you can add this person to your LifeNet.
- You're now free to take on a different opportunity—and it might be a better one!
- This rejection might be just the kick in the pants you needed to move on to something better. Think of rejection as a way of redefining your Comfort Zone.

Here are tips for handling rejection:

- Keep your eye on the big picture. If you stay focused on your goal, individual rejections will be easier to take.
- Don't second-guess yourself: Just because one person rejected you does not mean you're wrong.
- Tap into your passion and your patience in the face of repeated rejection. Remember, salespeople prepare for failure rates that can reach as high as 97%!

Rejection offers opportunity, yes, but that doesn't mean we need to seek it out. Remember these tips for avoiding rejection:

- Get a LifeNet referral before meeting with someone.
- Ask someone in your LifeNet to request a meeting for you.
- Use my theory of yes conditioning to encourage the person to say yes!

- Do your due diligence: Know exactly what the company is looking for and make sure you're meeting with the right person.
- Listen before speaking. Respond to the other person's needs, not yours.
- Admit to any potential problems up front and offer solutions.

Instead of perceiving rejection as a personal slap in the face, you now realize that when people say no, it's a sign that you can dig deeper, extending the conversation to find out how to improve your product or service. Then you can simply move on to the next opportunity.

Now that you understand rejection and how to manage it, you're well on your way to adopting the behaviors and strategies millionaires use all the time! But you still might have some practical questions about how to get your project up and running. Read on!

· 10 ·

Getting Out from Under

At this point in the book, you may be thinking, "Jen, this is all well and good, but how do I get started? I've only got $2,000 in savings—how can I fund my dream with that?" Or "This all sounds great, but I'm $20,000 in debt. There's no way I'll ever dig myself out from under that, let alone find the money to get started on my own business." Even if you're not starting your own business but trying to move toward the Millionaire Zone via your career track, too much debt will hold you back.

These are very common situations for many Americans today. When the national savings rate is negative and households with a credit card owe on average nearly $9,200, according to cardweb.com®, you know that real people are stuck somewhere in the middle of all that.

Well, rest easy. It'll take some work, but these obstacles do *not* mean you'll never reach the Zone. You just need to plan your journey carefully.

We'll start by showing you how you can find the money you

need to start your venture or push your career higher. There are some very common types of assets you can tap. Then I'll give you detailed tips on coping with debt. Finally I'll tell you the story of Kristine Burns, whom I met on the television show *Dr. Phil*. She came to me with $40,000 in credit-card debt. After following my strategy for getting out of debt, she now has a chance to get on the road to the Millionaire Zone.

Example from the Millionaire Zone
Warren Buffett, legendary investor, chairman, Berkshire
   Hathaway
No. 2 on Forbes 400
Net worth: $40 billion
Key strategy: Funding your trip to the Millionaire Zone

If you think there's no way you'll ever be able to get your venture off the ground, just think about Warren Buffett. The famous "sage of Omaha" started his company with just $100 of his own money, plus $105,000 from seven of his friends and family members.

There's no doubt Buffett offers wise counsel to those of us trying to move up in our financial lives. "You ought to be able to explain why you're taking the job you're taking, why you're making the investment you're making, or whatever it may be," Buffett said in a 1991 lecture to students and faculty at Notre Dame. "And if it can't stand applying pencil to paper, you'd better think it through some more."

Of course, few of us start off life with the kind of business acumen that Buffett has always had. One story relates how, when he was just six years old, Buffett bought a six-pack of Coca-Cola from his uncle for 25 cents, and re-sold the bottles for five cents each, collecting a tidy little profit of five cents. By the time he was 11 he was trading stocks, and at 14 he bought his first piece of land.

But if that's not the story of your childhood, don't worry. We can't all be one of the richest men in the world. Then again, what's stopping us?

CHAPTER CHECK-IN: Tapping Into Your Assets

You might be able to fund your venture using:

* Savings and investments
* Retirement accounts
* Jewelry, other personal possessions
* A future inheritance received today

But you'll need to consider the risks versus the rewards of this strategy.

Using What You've Got

So you've got a passion, and you'd love to put it into action using the strategies I've outlined in this book, but you're worried about finding the money to get it off the ground.

First, let's take a snapshot of your net worth. That means your assets (everything you own) and your liabilities (everything you owe).

Exercise: What's Your Net Worth?

Let's first take a look at some common types of assets.

Savings and Investments. The typical American has most of his/her savings sitting in checking or savings accounts, earning a paltry 1% to 3%. When you include fees and inflation, you're actually losing money. Those accounts are a good place to look for money to fund your venture or invest harder.

Take a close look at the interest you're earning on your savings and investments and at the money you expect to earn in your new venture. Does it match up? Can you earn more by putting your

Your Net Worth

Assets (current value)	You	Your Spouse	Total
Cash			
Checking			
Savings			
Money Market Accounts			
CDs			
Life Insurance (cash value)			
Other			
Sub-Total			
Retirement Accounts			
IRA/Roth IRA			
Pension/Profit Sharing			
401(k), 403(b), 457			
SEP/Keoghs			
Annuities (surrender value)			
Other			
Sub-Total			
Other Investments			
Stocks			
Bonds			
Mutual Funds			
Government Securities			
Land/Property			
Business			
Receivables			
Trusts			
Other			
Sub-Total			
Personal Property			
Home			
Second/Rental Home			
Car			
Household Items			
Jewelry			
Antiques/Collectibles			
Boat/Mobil Home/Etc.			
Other			
Sub-Total			
TOTAL ASSETS			

Liabilities (total debts you owe)	You	Your Spouse	Total
Outstanding Taxes Due			
College Loans			
Back Alimony Owed			
Back Child Support Owed			
Home Mortgage(s)			
Business Loans			
Personal Loans			
Home Equity Loans			
Credit Card Debt			
Other			
TOTAL LIABILITIES			

Final Calculation	You	Your Spouse	Total
Total Assets			
Subtract Total Liabilities			
NET WORTH			

money into your venture? How much do you believe in your concept? How long will it take to recoup your money?

Retirement Accounts. Do you have money saved in a 401(k)? That's another resource to consider, because often (but not always) you can borrow from your 401(k). You'll have to check with your employer to see whether your plan allows this. If it does, the maximum amount you can borrow is the total amount in the 401(k) up to $50,000.

Borrowing from your 401(k) might provide you with exactly what you need to get your venture off the ground. But many financial planners warn against borrowing from your retirement accounts. Why? When you borrow, your 401(k) administrator actually sells your investment shares to fund your loan; in essence, your money is no longer invested so you lose the tax-deferred compounded growth of your money. If, at the same time, you stop contributing to your 401(k), you might also miss out on free money in the form of employer contribution matches. But, just because you borrow doesn't mean you have to stop contributing.

Another thing to consider is that you must repay your 401(k) loan within five years. The good news on that score is that the interest rate is much lower than you'll find on any credit card, and you're paying *yourself* that interest.

Another option that often makes sense especially for those in their late 40s or 50s is to withdraw money from an IRA. Most people know of the rule that if you take out that money as a lump sum before the age of 59^1/$_2$, you'll get hit with a 10% penalty plus income taxes. But the law allows anyone before that age to take it out without the penalty so long as they receive the money in substantially equal payments each year. Check with your tax advisor on what amount you might qualify for.

Here's one question to consider when trying to assess whether borrowing or withdrawing from your IRA or 401(k) is right for you. If you take the money out, do you expect to reap a higher return than you would by keeping the money in mutual funds at 10% growing on a tax-deferred basis (even though studies show that average investors' returns trail the market miserably)? Do you have alternatives that won't deplete this important savings vehicle? Chances are, yes!

Risks Versus Rewards

To decide whether to pull money out of your savings or retirement accounts, you need to think about the risk/reward tradeoff. You need to figure out how much of your money you are willing to risk. It could be $5,000, $10,000, or $100,000. You also need to carefully budget your venture to calculate what your initial outlay will be. If, after running through the amount you were willing to risk, you have no buyers, no business, you need to write that money off to a life lesson, and move on.

Another part of the equation is to understand your own tolerance for risk. We all have a different sense of "how far am I willing to go?" You may think that starting your own venture is "riskier" than leaving your money in a savings account (pretty much anything you do with your money is riskier than an FDIC-insured savings account!). But think about the big picture risks like "risk of *career*," "risk of *lifestyle*," and "risk of *happiness*." In making your decision to read this book to begin your journey to a better life, you already weighed the relative importance of those "risks" of taking control of your future versus the "safety" of not doing anything. When you think about risking a few thousand dollars compared to having the chance to enter the Zone and manage your destiny, you can see the risk/reward equation changing in your favor.

Weighing the difference between the risk of pouring money into your own venture versus the risk of keeping money in your savings account is a lot like comparing stocks and bonds. Stocks are riskier because they represent an investment in the *equity* of a company. Bonds are an investment in the *debt* of a company. Equity holders are repaid *after* debt holders if the company ever goes bankrupt. That's why they get higher returns on average over time (9%) than bonds (5%). Venture capital, which is typically money invested as equity in start-up businesses, demands a much higher return than either stocks or bonds. This is because the risk associated with those businesses is so much greater than either equity or debt of larger, more established companies. If you were to invest your own money in someone else's venture, you'd want a higher return than what you could get in stocks or mutual funds.

The tradeoff looks like this:

	Risk	Average Annual Return
Venture	Highest	22.7%
Stocks	High	8.7%
Bonds	Low	5.3%
Savings	Lowest	3%

Source: National Venture Capital Association and Morningstar for the 10 years ending July 31, 2006.

Tax-Free Gifts and Other Creative Options

Finally, check your personal balance sheet again. Are there any less liquid assets that might work to fund your venture, things like jewelry, art, or antiques? Who knows? Maybe you have jewelry or old art that's worth something that, if sold, could help you get started. Maybe a relative has something they're looking to dump that might actually be worth something. Begin to open your eyes to the possibilities right in front of you.

If you're paying any serious money in rent or housing, consider either renting out a room or moving in with relatives. I did exactly that to keep my college debt down. You'd be amazed at how quickly you can save a few thousand dollars during the time you're planning your venture.

If you expect any inheritance money, consider seeing if there's a way to get even a portion of it now. As of 2006, gifts up to $12,000 can be given to individuals free of taxes. Often, a person who's interested in leaving you some money will be happy to give it to you earlier than planned as long as they don't need the money to live on. You'll want to make a good case that the money's going toward a worthy purpose, such as securing your financial future.

Another option is to suggest your relative contribute to a 529 college savings program, allowing you to take classes to sharpen your management and other skills. Contributions to a 529 plan grow tax-free and can be used at any accredited college. In addition, under IRS rules, a donor can contribute in one year up to five times the gift tax exclusion or up to $60,000 free of gift taxes ($120,000 for a married couple). Either way, there are some other important benefits in giving to you today, whether directly or through a 529:

- Lower estate taxes. Remember, your grandparents or other loved ones will pay hefty estate taxes of as much as 45% on estates over $2 million, minus any debts they owe upon death (these figures hold for people who pass in 2007 but are subject to change). By passing on some of their assets to you today, your relatives may lower their taxable estate.
- Enjoyment. A loved one who provides funding to you gets to experience the joy, while they're still with you. What is the point in waiting until they're gone?
- A worthy cause. A relative who's financially supportive can give knowing it is going toward a worthy cause, rather than toward things like toys and cars.

CHAPTER CHECK-IN: More Ways to Fund Your Venture

We've talked about using savings, investments, and retirement accounts to fund your venture. Other ways include:

- Carving money out of your paycheck
- Tax refunds and other lump sums

- Borrowing on your credit card (this is fraught with potential problems)
- Taking out a bank loan
- Turning to your LifeNet for start-up funds
- Tapping into your home equity

Carving Out Your Paycheck

Another source of cash for your venture is to sock away a portion of your paycheck. Take a portion that you'd normally be spending on nonessentials, or that you usually stash into savings. Choose a specific amount monthly and have it automatically invested in your own "venture fund" savings account. Just $200 a month could give you $2,400 in a year—definitely enough to get a prototype or test going. A separate account is important since you'll need to have clear records to track your spending for your venture from Day One.

Along the same lines, any bonuses you might be expecting from work or other unexpected lump sums like insurance proceeds or tax refunds might be directed into that account.

You also might think about doing freelance or consulting work on the side, then stashing that extra income away, solely to be used for your venture.

When You Ain't Got Much, Should You Borrow?

I've already shown you how real people have taken just $5,000 or $10,000—and even much less—and turned it into millions. You can combine your savings with *careful* use of personal borrowing to finance your dreams. But borrowing requires planning and discipline, because the downside to overleveraging yourself is obvious and painful. With proper caution, you can make your money go a long way.

Multimillionaire Bob Lorsch used credit cards to fund some of his initial ventures, as have others before him. This can work, but *proceed very carefully* if you go this route. Credit-card debt, with its often astronomical interest rates, can be addictive.

Consider Dale Swain. Dale's credit was shot to pieces after he racked up $230,000 in debt to start his own computer business, a company which ultimately failed. Still, after having spent more than a decade as a mechanical engineer at one company, Dale knew he was sick and tired of the office politics involved in working for someone else.

So he decided to try another venture. This one also required some start-up funds. Luckily, it was just $750. Still, because his credit limits were so low due to his poor credit history, Dale had to use four credit cards to charge that $750.

This second venture proved well worth the cost. Dale is now pulling in an average of $12,000 a month, selling health-care products online.

Again, credit cards can be hazardous to your financial health. For one, it's your personal credit at stake, so if the business goes belly up and you have $20,000 in credit-card debt, you'll have a tough monthly load to handle.

Credit-card interest rates can easily run as high as 30%. That's pretty steep and can lead you down a terrible spiral if you ever get stuck in the "minimum payment trap." Still, many people consider that a worthwhile risk when the alternative is bringing in investors who would demand an equity ownership in your business.

Heading to the Bank

A bank loan can be a great way to fund your venture. The rates on these loans are much lower than credit cards, usually about 10%, depending on the prime rate. And, you aren't giving up ownership in your company. But that doesn't mean they're easy to get. Remember Kevin DiCerbo?

Kevin spent a lot of time looking for funding to get his skin-care treatment company off the ground. After meeting with dozens of banks, Kevin did eventually succeed, but it took incredible persistence. He shopped tirelessly for a loan when he had no assets, not even a home, to pledge as collateral. His persistence paid off. His share of the firm is now worth millions of dollars.

Before you approach just any bank, you should start with *your* bank. They know you better than anyone else and will usually see the value of keeping you as a long-term customer. Still, you'll need a written business plan that details your approach to growing your business. A business plan is a roadmap for investors. It tells them two important things: a) the logic behind your venture as an investment and b) your thinking and philosophy as a manager of this venture. Unfortunately, the subject of business plans is a book in itself, but you can get more help at my Web site, www.themillionairezone.com.

Just remember that you'll be in a better position to get a bank loan if you have property as collateral for the loan. Also, be aware that until your business has consistent revenue and profitability to stand on its own, you will have to personally guarantee the loan.

If you have a relationship with a specific lending officer at your bank, great. Banks are always looking to expand relationships with existing customers. If not, start one. Start with the most senior officer you can find, usually the branch manager, and introduce yourself. Tell him or her that you've been a long-time depositor with X number of accounts and Y balances. You want to begin a personal loan relationship with a bank that appreciates its customers and is also interested in a long-term relationship. Sweeten the pot by telling him you will bring your various accounts, including your (and your spouse's, if you're married) retirement, investment, and 401(k) accounts as well as your mortgages and insurance. Many people don't realize this, but banks are now offering programs to encourage you to "bring it all home."

Reaching Out to Your LifeNet

Your LifeNet will be your most important resource in getting your venture off the ground.

Partners. Partners from your LifeNet can put in sweat equity to help get the business going. Sweat equity means your partner is contributing some value in the form of work, expertise, or qualifying leads, without being paid in cash, but in exchange for some type of ownership interest.

Many of the millionaires profiled in this book have family members who work for them (of course, once you're able you'll want to start paying these people!). Stuart and Stephanie Liner, for instance, work as a team. So do Wayne Finkel and his wife, Charlene Rios, who own the auditing firm. Susan Johnson, head of Susan's Healthy Gourmet, has her husband and her daughter working for her, while Erica Zohar's husband works with her, just to name a few examples.

Strategic Partners. A strategic partner is usually a company in the same line of business as your own whose business objectives are aligned with yours. This is a strategy I used for my first venture. I raised money from an executive with an online insurance marketplace that offered insurance quotes. They were going to be my partner anyway, but they were also looking to enjoy the rewards of a successful new company. Strategic partners are good candidates to team up with because, besides being established, they are already familiar with your industry, and maybe even you. Some will have a head of business development or strategy that may be looking for new opportunities, or consider the business line that can use your product or service. A strategic partner doesn't have to be a big corporation, by the way. The woman who started the medical transcription business in Chapter 7 could have taken it to a physician. In many ways, the job development program was a strategic partner to Desma, ensuring she had customers when she opened the doors to her resale store. All it takes to be an effective strategic partner is to have someone aligned with your interests, in the same business line, with more resources and contacts than you can presently bring to the table.

Investors. Many entrepreneurs seek equity investors who provide capital for a certain amount of ownership in the company. Other investors may be more interested in a fixed return on their investment, say, a 15% annual return.

There are two kinds of investors in start-ups. *Angel investors* are high-net-worth individuals looking to invest in new or young companies. You can find these people through special groups of angel investors or just individually—perhaps you or someone you know knows of a wealthy individual. *Venture capital* firms (VCs) are companies organized and funded specifically to invest other people's money (and being willing to risk their own—skin in the game!) in new or growing ventures. Many angel investors and VCs are located together in regions that are supportive of new businesses. In many cases, these investors will only invest in new ventures located right in their backyards, so you'll need to check. Both investor groups will often have a Web site describing their preferred investments with an online application process. Either way, you will definitely want to leverage your LifeNet to get to these groups.

VC firms often want to see a 30% to 40% annualized return on their money, so your business plan would need to demonstrate that. They also want to know you've committed your own money and/or sweat equity (your time!). There are thousands of VC firms, many of which operate in specific industries, so do your homework. Unlike the dot-com days when venture capitalists would throw money at you based on the strength of your ideas alone, today you need to demonstrate that your concept is viable. The best way to do that is to have customers, even if just as part of a test. VC firms will often demand a 50% ownership of your company. But the further along you are in demonstrating success, the less you may have to give up to get their money.

CHAPTER CHECK-IN: *Home Sweet Home Mortgage*

There are a variety of ways to tap into the value of your home to fund your venture, but each should be considered carefully before moving ahead:

- Obtain a second mortgage, either a home equity line of credit or a second home loan.

FUNDING YOUR TRIP TO THE MILLIONAIRE ZONE

	Savings	Home	Equity of Ownership Partner	Bank Loan	Credit Card	Friends/Family	Strategic Partner	Angel Investors	Venture Capital
Definition	The dough in your bank, savings or investment account	Use equity in home through a refinancing or line of credit	Someone who joins you in building the company; they typically get a share of ownership in the company	Bank provides a business loan at a fixed or variable interest rate, which must be paid back over a certain period of time; rates vary from 7-10%	The plastic you are so familiar with, with interest rates as high as 18-25%	Often the first source of money to initially start your venture; they get ownership. Future investors like to see that people who know you have put money in; typical amounts raised range from $5,000-$200,000.	Often, a company that would benefit by using your service/product (even your past employer); they may put up all or part of the money to build it if they get to use it first. They may also get ownership in the venture.	Already financially successful people who invest personal money into very young companies in exchange for ownership at some percentage level; they like to see that the venture has a few customers at least; angel groups invest $200,000-$1 million typically, individuals the same or less.	Professional investment firms that put money into companies ranging from start-ups to larger companies in exchange for ownership; you generally must have already proven that your business venture is successful, even if on a small scale; typical investments range from $1 million to $100 million.
Pros	You maintain entire ownership of the business	Low rates of 5-7%; interest is usually tax deductible; quick to access	Reduces your financial contribution; partner fills gaps in skills/knowledge	You maintain ownership	You maintain ownership	Quick access to money	Serves as your first customer and thus proves your success; may provide valuable expertise, resources, and introductions to help you grow. You may charge them as you would other customers.	Can provide valuable expertise and mentoring to you as these are experienced professionals and entrepreneurs themselves	Can raise substantial amount of money to take business to next level; brings credibility to the business
Cons	Reduces retirement nest egg	Higher monthly payments; home is at risk if unable to make payments	May not be able to make decisions unilaterally; you own less of the company	You personally guarantee the loan	High interest rates; you must make a personal guarantee until the business is able to support itself	These are people you know so if you fail and lose their money, you have to live with that	They often have ownership in the company, reducing your say	Sometimes difficult to obtain but if business is tested or proven	If given enough ownership in the company, can take over the business and kick you out (though you maintain your ownership)

- Use your home as collateral for a commercial loan.
- Sell your home.
- Rent out a room or your whole home to produce income.

Using Your Home to Get to the Millionaire Zone

A record number of families borrowed over a trillion dollars by tapping into their home equity in 2005. This is an appropriate strategy in some situations but not for most people. Why? Because instead of using the money for legitimate, well-reasoned wealth-building activities, people usually use their valuable home equity to buy more consumer goods, or they use the money to pay off debt—without a spending plan to make sure they stay out of debt.

So, think very carefully before using it to fund your venture, because if you lose it you lose not only the money it represents, but also the roof over your head. For more help specifically on getting the right loans, visit me at www.winningadvicelending.com.

That's the disclaimer. Now, read on.

A second mortgage. You could take out a second mortgage or home equity line to fund your venture. If you've owned your home for the last five years, chances are you've built up some nice equity. You may be able to tap into it in one of two ways:

1) You can personally borrow against the equity with a home equity line of credit—or HELOC in industry parlance—then inject the proceeds into the business. The pros of this strategy are that you control how much you want to borrow, rates are generally lower than a bank loan, and you're not giving up ownership. The cons, however, are that you will have higher monthly payments and, worst of all, you could lose your home if you can't make the payments.

A HELOC makes sense as a ready credit card though at much lower, tax-deductible interest rates (lines of credit hover around 7% to 8% versus 20% or more for a credit card, which is not tax deductible). Up to $100,000 is usually tax deductible, and there's no cost to open up a line of credit. Wayne and Charlene Finkel took out a home equity line to make sure they had money to meet payroll at those times when customers were late paying their bills.

A HELOC is one type of second mortgage. Another type is the home equity loan. This is structured more like a traditional mortgage. This type of loan makes sense if you need to borrow a significant amount, such as $100,000 or more, and if you plan to repay over a longer period of time. There are costs to finance this loan, usually about 1%, or $1,000 for every $100,000 you borrow. This type of loan typically makes sense only if you plan to stay in the home at least five years.

2) Another option is to use your home as collateral for a commercial loan. You can take out a low interest rate bank or SBA loan using your home or other property as collateral. Check with your state (such as the treasurer or commerce department) about special loans for businesses without any history, sometimes referred to as "capital access loans." The advantages are that you build credit in your company's name, and don't have to give up any ownership in your company. The downsides are that you'll pay a higher interest rate than with a home loan or line of credit, and you must personally guarantee the loan. As with a HELOC or home equity loan, you could lose the property if you can't make the payments.

Sell your home. Another way to use your home to your advantage is by selling it. If you need the cash and believe your business venture will appreciate more than your home would, this is an option. There are numerous entrepreneurs who have done just that and moved to lower cost, pro-business states to follow their dream.

Kevin's skin-treatment company is on track to post $5 million in annual sales this year and net $800,000 in profit. But a couple of years ago, when he was first starting out, Kevin was cash-poor. Kevin decided to rent rather than buy a home, he says, "because I believe in my own ability to do better with my money and I don't view my home as an investment."

Here's why Kevin's thinking can make sense for some people. Let's say he could afford to buy a $350,000 home. The down payment—money that would come out of his savings—is about $70,000 and the monthly payment is about $1,500. Over five years, assuming his house increases in value 10% each year—which is not unlikely in Los Angeles, where he lives—Kevin's investment in his house would generate about $250,000 after broker fees and after the loan payoff, for an average annual return on his down payment of 29%. And in most areas of the country, his return would be lower, given that housing values rise less steeply.

Instead, Kevin prefers to pay $1,600 a month in rent for a house of the same size. While he's not enjoying the tax benefits of a home loan, he is able to use his cash—the $70,000—for his business. And so far, Kevin is right. In just two years, his portion of his business is now worth $5 million, far more than he would have ever gained by tying it up in his house.

Kevin believed he could do better, based on his passion and his research into the business. "I knew the business had legs," he says. "I saw a need for this service, a need for a brand, and a financial opportunity. I saw the margins were high, people were willing to pay a lot, and the industry is growing at 15% a year."

Your home as an income machine. Another way to tap into the value of your home is to use your home as an income-generating source. That is, rent out a room or rent out the whole home at a rate high enough to cover the mortgage. Then, rent out a smaller apartment or condo for yourself and use the savings for your venture. Or, do like Mark Fitzgerald did if you have a multi-unit rental property or are considering investing in one: stay in one unit and rent out the others to, hopefully, cover the full payment on the loan.

Do this for just a year or two until your venture gives you the income you need.

Going from Nothing to the Millionaire Zone

So, let's say all the numbers over $1,000 are on the liability side of your balance sheet. How do you go about getting on the road to the

Millionaire Zone? Kristine Burns is a great example of how to go from overwhelming debt and little or no assets, to a fresh start. Kristine and I met on the *Dr. Phil* show. She was suffocating under $40,000 in credit-card debt. Kristine is a single mother with a 9-year-old daughter, Kayla, so she's not supporting just one but two, and gets no financial support. As part of his program, Dr. Phil asked me to look at her assets and recommend solutions to her financial difficulties. She had zip—no savings, little in her teachers' retirement account, no equity in her home thanks to a horrendous variable-rate loan.

Kristine was holding down three jobs. She's an elementary school teacher, she works at a pizza parlor, and she does tutoring on the side.

Her strength and passion is teaching, so her most obvious option was to expand her tutoring business. There is tremendous demand for good tutors as the need for quality education at all ages is being driven by our increasingly competitive society. And, it's more lucrative than any other option she has: She can make $40 an hour, and she can increase that income exponentially in the following ways:

- Create a compelling name for her business (I suggested Tutor Today USA), create a simple Web site, and post flyers at schools. Conduct interviews in local parent magazines and newspapers to generate business.
- If she doesn't have the money for a Web site (though she can set one up for just $50 at Yahoo or other Web portals), she could partner with someone in her LifeNet whose expertise is Web sites and online marketing and give them a piece of the business. That person should be responsible for building the site and getting it in local online listings.
- To expand even further, the two could develop some online tutoring programs, perhaps starting in one or two areas like math and English. The basic software is already out there so they don't have to reinvent the wheel.

- They can get an endorsement from Kristine's school as well as other schools in the area. Parents who have already hired Kristine to tutor their kids can provide references and can be detailed on the Web site and noted in any marketing materials.

Kristine could easily grow her business with just a couple hundred dollars. Once she shows just a little success, she and her partner might raise capital to expand further, perhaps going into other states or regions or testing some online marketing programs.

If Kristine wants to really think big, she could consider a national tutoring company. She might sell franchises that allow others to offer tutoring in their local areas under the name of Tutor Today USA. Kristine then would get upfront money for the franchise along with an ongoing share of revenues. This teacher is on her way to the Millionaire Zone.

Managing Your Debt to Create Savings

I'm guessing that debt is one of the biggest factors holding people back from turning their passions into profits. But, that fear doesn't have to stop you from reaching your financial goals. You simply need to manage it, as with anything else, to make room for your business venture.

In addition to re-negotiating Kristine's credit-card debt, we tightened up Kristine's spending and lowered her house payments so she can use the cash to start her tutoring business.

Kristine originally bought her house for $75,000. A few years ago, she refinanced her home mortgage to pay off debt, leaving her with a mortgage of $94,000. Unfortunately, the appraisal came in at only $105,000, which put her loan-to-value at 90%. That put her in a corner, since few other banks would refinance her with so little apparent equity.

This meant that when her adjustable loan, which had started at 4.5%, jumped to 8.75%, she was stuck. Her payments were only paying off interest, not reducing her principal, so she wasn't paying off any debt, let alone building wealth. Yikes!

After talking to various lenders to get her the best rate, we settled on a loan where her monthly payment would be $619, thanks to a 30-year fixed rate at 6.25%, lower than her original $700 variable-rate loan payment. When I called Kristine to tell her the good news about her new loan, she said, "I'm speechless, which for me is crazy. I am so excited it's ridiculous."

Kristine could now begin to save and use this money to print up flyers and get a simple Web site going.

CHAPTER CHECK-IN: Steps for Getting Out from Under

Now we discuss how to start managing your debt, so you can pay it off and get going on your path to the Zone!

- Take inventory.
- Create a new spending plan.
- Negotiate with your creditors.
- Kick a habit.
- Take a time-out.

Getting Out from Under

You're probably saying: "Fine. I'll refinance to a better home loan. But what about all my credit-card debt?"

I know it doesn't seem easy when you're living paycheck to paycheck, or you've been hit with a job loss or medical crisis. Trust me, I've counseled thousands, including dear family members going through those very same challenges. But I've learned from years of experience, and countless examples, that you can break the cycle and reach the Millionaire Zone if you put your mind to it. I'm going to repeat that because it's so important: *You can get out of debt and reach the Millionaire Zone if you put your mind to it.* Many successful millionaires have faced debt and have even filed bankruptcy, but they overcame because they believed in themselves.

Take a look at how we handled Kristine's $40,000 in credit-card debt.

Kristine was in . . . well . . . quite a mess. Not only did she have rates as high as 25%, but the credit-card companies were starting to come after her. And she had that horrible home equity line of credit that kept adjusting upward each month.

Her situation definitely needed a 9-1-1 call. Thanks to Dr. Phil, I was the financial doctor in this case! When Kristine put my advice into action, and saw that we were going to be able to get her out of debt and moving toward the Zone, she said, "I love you. I can't believe it! I'm so excited I'm telling all my friends."

Step 1: Take Inventory. The first thing Kristine and I did was to take a look at her net worth so we could see all her debts and any assets she had (no assets and tons of debt—not good!). Next, we looked at her income and expenses to track money coming in and money going out. She used my Quick & Easy Budget Kit and had her own "ah-ha!" moment.

"I saw that I'm paying property taxes and insurance. That made me think, 'Oh, my gosh!'" That's when Kristine really woke up to the fact that she's spending money on things that she wasn't even aware of.

Step 2: Create a New Spending Plan. I could see that Kristine was about $300 in the hole each month. The goal in this step is to see what Kristine—and you!—have left over after covering all *necessary* expenses.

You need to distinguish between what you *need* to spend each month and what's discretionary and could be cut. For instance,

Kristine admitted that her money was going to "toys for the dog and videos for her daughter." She could now see how her bad habits were preventing her from reducing her monthly debt burden, and stealing away time she'd rather spend with her daughter.

Take a long, hard look at your spending to see where you can cut back. Consider *everything* discretionary other than eating, basic clothing, and shelter. Everything else, as Dr. Phil said, is "on the table."

Let me put it bluntly. Your necessary expenses are gas, medical costs, mortgage or rent—but you'll need to leave out the money you spend on entertainment, eating out, vacations, and dog toys.

When you've detailed your necessary expenses, this list becomes the basis for your new spending plan. The next key strategy is to get on an easy spending program that prompts you to pay bills on time, set money aside to pay off debt, and keep track of overall spending. You can see our spending software, which helps you track your spending at any time, at www.winningadvice.com.

Step 3: Negotiate with Your Creditors. Kristine was on the brink of bankruptcy. Debt was just piling up with not enough income to support it, even though she worked at three jobs.

The first thing to remember about excess credit-card debt is that you have more clout than you think. The last thing a creditor wants you to do is to file bankruptcy. They would much rather get something from you than nothing. This gives you the room to negotiate with them.

Credit-card companies usually offer two debt remediation programs: forbearance or a repayment plan. A repayment program is designed to get you to pay off your debt over a certain period of time, usually five years. Under a repayment program:

- Your interest rate will be radically reduced, to as low as 1%.
- Your payments will remain the same, but the lower rate means you pay more of the principal, so you get out of debt sooner.
- You generally pay off your debt in five years.

- There is no added cost or fee for the program, unless you go through a third party, such as a credit counseling agency.
- It is generally for people in a serious situation, such as a job loss or with major medical expenses.

Credit-card companies and other creditors also usually offer forbearance, which is a suspension of payments for a period of time, usually a year, although interest continues to accrue. This is really just a breather for you to have more time to figure out a solution to your debt or to get more income. Generally, if you've got a really steep debt load, you want to use a repayment program.

How do you negotiate with creditors? It's not easy, and some creditors are more willing to work with you than others.

With Kristine, I negotiated with two credit-card companies on her behalf. On one credit card alone, where she was carrying a balance of more than $20,000, I saved her nearly $200,000 in interest and fees (assuming she continued making just minimum payments over some 30 years) by getting her on a debt repayment plan where her interest rate dropped from 25% to 4%.

I also negotiated away any late fees or penalties. While on the repayment plan, she can't use her credit card. Here's the result after we re-negotiated the terms of her $21,000 in credit-card debt on one credit card:

Kristine's Credit-Card Debt

	Before the Negotiation	After the Negotiation
Monthly payment	$420	$400
Interest rate	25%	4%
Late fees	$39	$0
Over-limit fees	$39	$0
Years to pay off	30 years	5 years
Total interest to be paid	$193,000	$3,000

Are you ready to try negotiating with your creditors? Be prepared to answer these questions:

- What are your monthly spending outlays and income? This shows what you have after covering necessary expenses.
- How much can you pay toward debt?
- Why did you get into debt? You want to have a very clear answer. Did you lose your job? Get hit with a medical disaster? Go through a divorce with no child support or alimony? These are all legitimate reasons, the kind that will usually lead to creditors helping you.

To ensure a successful outcome:

- Be confident. You hold the cards. There is every reason for them to cut a deal with you.
- Be clear and articulate.
- Know what you want.

This process can be pretty scary and intimidating. If you don't feel you can do it on your own, consider going to a credit counseling agency. They can be helpful assisting you with budgeting and may be able to negotiate with your creditors for terms that you cannot get on your own.

However, be careful. There are bad operators out there who charge steep up-front fees and throw you into a debt-management plan that may not be right for you. The IRS and other government agencies are investigating a slew of credit counseling agencies for not satisfying the "educational mission" required by their nonprofit status. Ask the agency how their counselors are trained (you want to work with counselors who've gone through some kind of certificate program on managing finances). Work with a credit counseling agency that offers you *at least* 20 minutes of counseling before they propose a plan that's right for you.

Other Ways to Get Out of Debt

1. Avoid the minimum-payment trap. Perhaps you don't feel your debt level is out of control, so you don't need to negotiate with creditors. But if you carry a balance of $5,000 on an 18.9% credit card, you will pay about $26,000 in interest costs over 13 years, assuming you only make the minimum payment of, in this case, $200 (minimum payments are now as much as 4% of your balance, thanks to new laws). If you transfer your balance to a lower rate card, say, one that charges 15%, but you continue making the minimum payment required by your previous card—$200 per month— you could cut your debt costs substantially. You would be out of debt in three and a half years (assuming no more charging!) and will have paid $3,200 in interest costs, a fraction of the original $26,000 under the first scenario.

Now, at the beginning of this book I said my strategy for getting into the Millionaire Zone isn't about scrimping and saving, so that you earn your first million after 30 years. But scrimping and saving is exactly what you have to do if you're trying to climb out from under a big pile of debt.

2. The Time-Out. I've also counseled couples and individuals facing difficult transitions, everything from divorce to coming out of the military with limited skills. In these situations, I sometimes suggest they take a "time-out" and go live with either set of parents to simply get on their feet, take the financial pressures away, and have time to regroup and develop a game plan.

Don't be embarrassed to ask for help from your LifeNet. Your parents would likely be glad to see that, with just a little help from them, in a year or two, you're out from under and on your way to the Millionaire Zone!

Strategy	Pros	Cons
Cut expenses, increase payments	No impact on credit	Still paying high interest rates
Kick a habit	Pay off debt quicker; live a more health-conscious life (free of caffeine, cancer, etc.)	Not as many lattes, cigarettes, or other vices
Shift payments from savings to debt	No impact on spending; better use of cash since you usually cannot get a return on your savings higher than the interest rate you're paying on debt	If you're not putting aside a lot in savings right now, it may take a long time to pay off debt
Consolidate to a lower-rate credit card	Can generate substantial savings, depending on your credit	Beware of credit-card companies that may later increase your initial rate
Negotiate with creditors (directly or via a credible credit counseling service)	Get substantially reduced interest rate and savings	May go on credit report, though usually temporarily; cannot use credit card
Borrow against home equity	Interest rate is a fraction of rate on credit cards; interest is tax deductible (making a 7% home equity loan about 5% after tax deduction); allows you to use cash	Studies show a majority who do this go back into debt (due to no spending plan); you may be "upside down" (owe more than it's worth) on home if housing market drops and you need to sell; may not have equity for building wealth or emergency
Borrow from family/friends	Debt paid off immediately; low to no interest paid; no impact on credit; can still use credit cards	Possible impact on important relation-ships if unable to repay

Six Ways to Eliminate Debt

Weighing Different Debt-Elimination Strategies

We've talked about ways to eliminate debt. On the previous page is a summary of the pros and cons of the different strategies for doing that. As you move toward the Zone, you will need to choose carefully which path you take to eliminate debt. For example, if you ruin your good credit and later want to take out a bank loan, you will have a tough time getting it.

The End Zone

Many Americans are laboring under a steep debt load with little in the way of savings. We've learned that there are myriad ways for you to find the money you need to start your venture:

- Savings and investments
- Retirement accounts
- Jewelry and other possessions
- Future inheritance received today
- Money carved out of your paycheck
- Tax refunds and other lump sums
- Loans from credit cards (with a big warning on this one)
- Bank loans
- Tap into your home equity
- Investors
- People and organizations in your LifeNet!

And here are strategies for paying off debt quickly. These are all related to actively managing your debt so you can take control over it—and eradicate it!

- Take inventory.
- Create a spending plan.

- Negotiate with your creditors.
- Kick a habit.
- Take a time-out.
- Avoid the minimum-payment trap.

Now you've got clear strategies for getting out from under that debt and moving yourself toward greater financial success. In our next chapter, we'll look at some common myths about making money. Are you beginning to see your path to the Millionaire Zone?

10 Things That Ain't So

The humorist Josh Billings once said, "It's better to know nothing than to know what ain't so."

Now that you've read this far, you're familiar with the grand misconception that millionaires are all self-made individuals who never had to rely on anyone else. As you now know, the people I've profiled in this book all have become successful and earned millions by using their LifeNets.

But there are other wrong-headed notions about how people get into the Millionaire Zone. This chapter debunks those popular beliefs, so that you don't make the same mistakes as you move toward your financial goals.

Myth 1: Not Rich in One Year? Time to Give Up

Rich in one year? The majority of entrepreneurs don't make it in their first year. That hardly means they've failed.

Like a successful weight-loss diet, my plan for getting you into the Millionaire Zone is not a quick fix. It's a life change. This is about building wealth for the long term.

Operating in the Millionaire Zone isn't just "I've made $1 million." It's the way you operate in the world, the way you approach everything that will increase your chances of success. So, focus on following the strategies in this book and realize that nothing worthwhile comes quick. There's always a process.

That process will vary depending on your situation. Businesses follow a variety of growth patterns and I've seen all kinds. They often follow a trajectory, taking several years to reach profitability. Some have a year of success, followed by a setback and then a year of success.

There are many roads to success, but the millionaires profiled in this book all talk about long-term planning as a key ingredient. Successful companies develop annual budgets and five-year plans so they know where they're headed. It allows them to focus on the day-to-day concerns of running a business, while still keeping an eye on the future. Once you have established long-term goals, you will make better short-term decisions—decisions that keep you on track to the Millionaire Zone.

Myth 2: Bigger Is Better

Closely connected to thinking that you need to be profitable in one year is the idea that your company has to be big to be successful. Many novice entrepreneurs envision grandiose growth plans, not realizing that sometimes it makes sense to scale back.

Take Ron Greitzer's situation. His carpet recycling company has gone through some tough times. Ron shared his problems with one group in his LifeNet—a forum of like-minded entrepreneurs who get together to provide mutual support to one another.

"I had one guy who pointed out, given my cost structure, that I had to get so much bigger just to break even," Ron says. "This guy said, 'Why don't you just consolidate and get smaller—and profitable!' I had never looked at it like that.

"I noodled on it for months," Ron said. "It didn't make sense to me at first. Then one day I was at a breakfast meeting with my chief financial officer and my father—he's my most trusted counsel. We were talking about other opportunities and what we needed to do. We worked out a plan on a napkin. It took 18 months to execute, but we changed the company."

As Ron's story shows, you may alter your plan as you test and learn, but always keep some kind of plan in motion. And sometimes, smaller is better.

Myth 3: Once Failed, Twice Shy

Starting a business isn't easy, and sometimes things go wrong. Does that mean you're just not meant to be an entrepreneur? Not at all. Many business owners who've built a seven-figure fortune got there only after failing at an earlier venture. Just as defining success is fundamental to any business plan, so is defining failure. Figure out by what measure you will decide when to throw in the towel. Is it dollars spent? Months or years devoted to a venture? The fifth time your spouse threatens to leave?

Like many members of the Millionaire Zone, Dale Swain got there only after failing with another business. He quit his job after 13 years as a mechanical engineer to start his own computer business—and ended up losing big.

"I laid out my game plan, studied that industry and did everything," Dale says, now looking back. "I just found out the hard way you can't compete with the Gateways and the Dells of the world. It was a disaster."

And sometimes you have to step back to move forward. "I'd definitely be worth more now if I had gone straight from my engineering position to the Integrity Group [Dale's current, very successful venture] working as an independent distributor, and skipping the computer business." But Dale points out that "some of my most valuable lessons came from the computer business. If I had *not* done that and failed, and learned from it, I probably wouldn't be as successful today."

One thing the pros all agree on is that too many people quit on the brink of making it. Dale almost gave up before realizing he was close to success with his current business. "It was late on a Friday," he says. "I had a call with a guy in California and I didn't even get three words in before he hangs up. I thought it must be a bad connection, so I called him back. And the guy just cussed me out. That was like the icing on the cake of an already tough week. I picked the phone up to put in my resignation to the parent company, but they were closed. By Monday I got my head on straight, and within a month I had a major rank advancement," Dale says, meaning he advanced in the company due to his sales success. "I was within 30 minutes of throwing the whole thing away."

As Dale learned, if you give up, you also give up all the powerful lessons you can learn, lessons which actually will bring you closer to the Millionaire Zone.

Myth 4: Bet the Ranch

Most successful people I've spoken to know how much they're willing to risk and don't go beyond that. Is it $5,000 or $50,000?

Erica Zohar went in willing to spend $10,000 and no more, to secure her first customer.

"It made all the difference knowing that I was not using my life savings," Erica says. "I didn't have all that pressure on my shoulders that if this doesn't work out, I've lost my home, lost everything."

Her strategy, she says, "is like going to Vegas and knowing in your head what you're willing to lose. Having that kind of mind-set made it a lot easier to accept the possibility of failure: 'If this doesn't work out, I'm going to go to the next thing.' Knowing how much you're willing to lose is very important. That's the problem with a lot of entrepreneurs. They're always looking at what they can make rather than what they're willing to lose."

Being willing to lose *something*, however—having "skin in the game"—is exactly what investors look for from prospective clients.

Wouldn't you rather put your money with someone who also has a significant stake? Who will work hard to protect and grow everybody's hard-earned money?

Myth 5: If It Doesn't Sizzle, It Will Fizzle

Frankly, lots of successful businesses aren't particularly exciting. In fact, they're often downright boring. But what *is* sexy is their cashflow, their high-profit margins, their simplicity or their scalability. That, my friends, is what will get you to the Millionaire Zone.

My friend Owen Glenn started a business some 20 years ago carrying cargo on ships across the oceans. Not a business I would call glamorous but today Owen is a billionaire. How about laundry bags? Definitely not sexy, but the brains behind this easily made product is the second largest seller of laundry bags to dry cleaners in the U.S.

Years ago when I worked for the California State Treasurer's Office, I visited a plant that made bolts used to produce airplanes; our office had financed them. As I walked around, I thought to myself *Bolts to make airplanes?* It didn't sound particularly exciting until I saw they were generating $5 million a year in revenues for a company owned by just two partners.

My friend Jason Feingold, barely 30, recently started a company selling power generators online. After just three months, he and his partner are raking in $100,000 a month, with sales doubling in the fourth month. Since they don't hold inventory—orders are sent directly to the manufacturers—expenses are low and the business is easy to manage. And it's easily scalable, meaning he can keep growing and expanding without significantly higher operating expenses.

For others, it can be just the sheer idea of winning that is a turn-on. Take Wayne Finkel's work in bank fraud. Like accounting, auditing is not likely to turn up on any reality shows. But Wayne loves it. "It's kind of like a game," he says. "Every time we win a new contract—it's like 'Yeah!' It's about having my own business and succeeding."

If it fills a need, plays a positive role in people's lives, and makes money, you'll have the thrill of a lifetime.

Myth 6: It's Only My Time

Too many people who start ventures focus on money, when they need to be concerned about their time as well. Let's say you leave your job and two years later still don't have your venture up. Not only have you lost whatever money you put into it, but you lost two years of earnings in your old job. Can you go back and make it up? No. You're out the time and the money. Losing your time—that is, not getting money in return for it—can actually be a bigger risk than your money.

Remember my friend Karlyn, from Chapter 7? She's starting a business to help consumers and small businesses navigate the insurance-claim system after catastrophes such as hurricanes and tornadoes. She's thinking about charging subscriptions, but may waste precious time trying to get paying customers, delaying profitability. What should she do? Use her time now to line up bigger companies who can afford to pay right away. I suggested, for instance, that she focus on insurance companies that are required by law to provide such services to their customers. That way, she'll have cash coming in and can take time to test whether individuals would be willing to pay for her service.

We also need to think about the value of our time when people ask us to spend it on their behalf. All of us have friends, relatives, you name it, who ask of our time in some way. Let's say your friend says to you, "Can you do me a favor and help my sister on a project? She can't pay you though." You think, "Okay, it's only my time." Well, it's more than that because your time is worth money! And while giving your time is an essential part of nurturing your LifeNet, make sure that both you and the beneficiary understand its value. In the same way, you need to value other people's time. For instance, when someone gives you time for a meeting, remember that his time is worth something, too. Respect people's time. Be on time for meetings. Confirm up front how much time the other person has for the meeting, and set the agenda so that you accomplish what you want to during the time you have. And make sure the other person also gets something valuable for his or her time.

Myth 7: "Good Enough" Is Good Enough

Someone once said that true customer service is what you do when no one is looking. It's that kind of quality in every aspect of my business that I strive for. You hear it from every successful person, whether they are a Forbes 400 member or enjoying a seven-figure fortune. The reason is obvious. All consumers have so many alternatives to choose from, the companies who consistently win are the ones who put product and service quality above all else. In this super competitive, global economy, cutting corners or compromising on what you deliver to the customer—and how you deliver it—just doesn't work. From the teller at the bank you see chewing gum to the CEO of a communications giant who doesn't know how to turn on his computer, it's the little things which—unattended—can really kill a good business.

The people I've interviewed have consistently said that their ability to execute or do a good job is what kept their customers returning. That means you need to set high standards, not just for yourself but for the people around you. You need to do what you say you're going to do. You need to put your best foot forward. When that happens, you'll feel more confident about your chances of success, because you won't have left any strings hanging that could lead to a failure or rejection.

What do we do when we're not up to being our best, maybe we're just feeling off, or we're troubled by a problem at home? "Even when you're at your worst, you need to put out as if you're at your best," says multimillionaire Bob Lorsch. Sometimes you need to manage expectations. "There are times when you just can't be at your best, but what I do is I tell the people I'm meeting, 'Hey, I'm not feeling well. I really appreciate your taking the time to get to know me,

and I apologize in advance if I say anything that isn't on point,' "
Bob says. Still, remember that you need to focus on being your
best. By putting on a smile, staying focused on the moment, and
remembering your financial dreams, you can make a meeting a
success.

Myth 8: It's Who You Know

This book is dedicated to the proposition that you can use the people you know in your LifeNet to help you get to the Millionaire
Zone. But your LifeNet is designed to open you up to the world of
possibilities, to people (and places and resources) you've never met,
or dreamed of meeting.

"I like to think there are no strangers; there are just friends and
contacts I haven't met." That variation on an old quote from Will
Rogers highlights my point that it's not who you know, it's who
you *don't* know who may in fact be the person most helpful to you.

I can point to countless times where, by using my LifeNet, I
found my way to someone, some partner, some company I didn't
know. When I assembled a group of advisors for my first company—
an advisory board to whom I could turn for advice—many were big-
name CEOs. Did I know them? Absolutely not. Did I use my LifeNet
to reach them and gain their support? Yes. And what a difference it
made. One became a member of my board of directors, bringing
more credibility to the company. Another was in a powerful video
we produced, which helped attract other recognized speakers. Still
another introduced me to potential investors.

Keep in mind, also, that the people you know may not always be
the right people for the job. You need to surround yourself with people who believe in you and who believe in your venture. They should
complement your strengths and weaknesses. For instance, if you're
not comfortable with financial statements, find someone who can
teach you or assist in putting together financial projections.

The person you need to know may seem unapproachable, but

that is often not the case. "When I see a person or an individual or an organization that I want to get to know, I'm not scared to pick up the phone and call the chairman or anyone on the board of directors," says Bob Lorsch. "In fact, when I want to find out about an organization, I go to the Internet. I search out who's management, from the CEO and the board members to senior vice presidents to vice presidents. Then I'll send an e-mail to people that I know who are in related industries. For example, right now I'm interested in meeting companies in medical technologies. I'll ask, 'Who do you know at WebMD?' and I'll send that to everybody I know in information technologies and somebody surely will know somebody on the list," he says.

Like Bob, those who reach the Millionaire Zone go where they need to get a faster decision or the support they need. If you go in with the feeling that someone is "better" or more important than you, you need to change that perception. Poet Maya Angelou once said to me that to succeed in life you "must see yourself as valuable, no less than the CEO of the firm and no more than the babysitter whom you pay. But equally, a full human being." She went on to say, "And if you have some confidence, it is likely that an employer will look to you with more felicity, more warmth, more respect. And people feel, then, I can be safe here. This person is really going to look after my affairs." This applies to virtually anyone—not just a prospective employer but a partner, a prospective customer, a prospective advisory board member.

Let's say Raymond is trying to turn his special cheese-flavored pretzels into profits. He could send out an e-mail to his LifeNet to see whether anyone knows someone at the airlines, so he can pitch his pretzels as a passenger snack. He could also show up at a conference in his city, where the CEO of Jet Blue is speaking. Which strategy should Raymond choose? Both. If you start at the top and get support, everybody below will be on board. If you start at the bottom or in the middle, it will take longer to reach the decision-maker, but you may also discover some valuable insights into the behavior of the company you might not get from someone higher up. A favorite trick of an investment banker I know is to get to know the secretary or administrative assistant to the CEO. The assistant will often know more about what's going on than anyone, and can help you gauge the optimum time to speak with his or her boss.

In any case, your LifeNet is often the means of reaching someone you don't know who can otherwise make something happen for you—faster, better.

Myth 9: Don't Count Your Chickens

We're all superstitious to some extent. It's in our nature not to tempt fate by predicting our successes or assuming accomplishments. To get to the Zone, however, you need to fight that urge. You need to act as if what you want to happen is already in progress.

There are two reasons for this. First, it's important to behave to the world as if your vision is already being realized so that you get focused on that goal. If you approach people with the attitude that your venture will take off "one day," it sounds pie-in-the-sky. From Day One, you should be talking as if it is *already happening*, as if it's up and running and successful. By acting committed and winning, you will be committed and winning.

I remember when I first met Phil Burruel, a former policeman and now a millionaire himself. He told me that a company was interested in his security software product. "When we sign them up," he told me, "we'll have 10,000 computers using our program." I really heard that *when*. No "ifs." Phil was still in the pitching stages, but he was focused on the goal of getting that deal. I could see how the people who worked with him were also adopting his attitude, and *making things happen* as a result.

The second reason you need to act as if your chickens are hatching is that to survive in the early stages of your venture, you need to get investors, customers, and suppliers excited about a product that may not even exist yet. You are selling people on things that haven't even happened!

That's okay. It happens all the time. While your product may exist only on paper, you need to have the relationships and resources in place to execute quickly should a prospect say, "We need it next week."

One final word on the idea of acting "as if." Erica Zohar always refers to her company as "we." Even back when it was just Erica and no employees, she used "we" to imply a company that was already successful, already growing. Language has a huge effect on perception. Use the power of positive language to sell yourself and your business—and keep counting those chickens.

Myth 10: Wait Until You've Reached the Millionaire Zone to Give Back to Society

You don't have to—and you shouldn't—wait until you're a millionaire before you begin giving to charitable causes. Philanthropy is a skill like anything else. It needs to be practiced as early in your life as possible. No matter how small the sums may be, getting into the habit of giving to others is important if it's going to become a life-long practice. Even if you don't have the money to give, you can volunteer your time on the weekends or in the evenings. You could become a mentor to someone who aspires to great achievements as you did at that age. You can provide an internship for a college student who needs practical work experience to build up their resume.

There are many wonderful examples of giving back. I remember reading about a young man who hires disabled people in his venture; he gives back by hiring people who would otherwise be out of work. And look at the giving back Ron Greitzer does by helping the environment through his carpet recycling business.

For others, the goal is to start a dream organization or simply contribute to a favorite cause now. For instance, my friend Maryanne donates to end children's hunger to educate her own children about their good fortune. Just remember: You don't have to wait to give back until you're retired. You can start right now.

The End Zone

Congratulations—by reading this far you've taken a huge step in reaching your financial goals! In Chapter 12, I'll give you a step-by-step 30-Day Getting Started Program that will move you even closer to that place you want to be: the Millionaire Zone.

· 12 ·

Getting to the Millionaire Zone: Your Zone Profile and 30-Day Getting Started Program

Congratulations! I hope by now you feel you've learned a great deal! Most important, you've learned that you don't have to go it alone, and that, in fact, thousands who have come before you didn't. Rather, they used their LifeNets to propel them into the Millionaire Zone.

So where do you go from here? Now that you have all these tools at your disposal, how do you know which path to take to make the kind of money you know you're worth—the kind of money that will allow you to fulfill your personal dreams?

I can tell you from my own life experience, and talking with thousands of Americans, that choosing the path can itself be a challenge. There are as many choices as there are readers of this book. You can start a business, invest in real estate, invest in stocks, partner with an existing company, start an online business, move to the top ranks of the company for which you work. But which is right for you? How can you best apply the LifeNet principles and put yourself closer to the Millionaire Zone?

In this chapter, I lay out the first steps to creating your LifeNet and heading toward the Millionaire Zone with a 30-Day Getting Started Program.

First, to help you figure out which path makes sense for you, let me tell you about my proprietary Millionaire Zone Profile. I'm making it available both to you *and* your friends to keep with our theme of tapping into the people, places, and resources around you.

Get Your *Free* Millionaire Zone Profile

Visit www.themillionairezone.com

The Millionaire Zone Profile

Many Americans are confused about how they should go about making money; it's one reason they never move forward financially. To help you, I've created the Millionaire Zone Profile. If you've ever taken a personality test, you'll notice some similarities. My program, however, is unlike anything else out there.

When it comes to determining which path you should take to make money, there are four capacities to consider: personality, financial, risk, and time. I've developed 50 key questions that allow us to measure your responses and place you on one of four primary paths. These paths are designed to serve as your compass, setting you off in a direction based on the answers to these questions.

What are the kinds of things we look for within these four factors?

- Personality: How does your personality come into play? Do you like working for others or yourself? Do you have the persistence and drive to make it to the Millionaire Zone?
- Financial capacity: What financial resources do you have to help you reach the Millionaire Zone?

- Risk: Where are you on the risk spectrum? You'll fall somewhere between the extremes of daredevil and couch potato.
- Time: How much time do you have to devote to getting to the Millionaire Zone right now? Are you in a full-time job that absorbs most of the working day but leaves weekends free, or are you a stay-at-home mom who would like full- or part-time work?

Through a series of questions, the Millionaire Zone Profile will place you in one of four Millionaire Zone Paths to help you understand the most appropriate financial route for you to build your wealth. It could be leaving your job to start a business, getting a venture going on the side while keeping your job, investing in high-risk start-ups or real estate while remaining in your job, or simply investing more intelligently. While the Profile is *not* designed to be a complete analysis of your financial picture or offer specific investment advice, it will give you an overall sense of your money style and provide money-making ideas based on the answers you've provided. From there, you can follow my 30-Day Getting Started Program outlined below.

It's designed to be easy and fun. Most important, you can achieve what thousands of others before you have, simply by not going it alone.

I believe that my LifeNet approach to the Millionaire Zone gives more Americans the chance to make their first million than any other "get rich" method. The concept of redefining your Comfort Zone and using your Home Zone to allow you to feel more secure and more confident as you follow your personal drivers—and leveraging your LifeNet as you go—is an extremely compelling one. Unlike any other program, it uses the people, places, and resources around you to help you build your business, your fortune, and your life.

My LifeNet approach has been used by thousands of very successful entrepreneurs, including me. It can easily be applied by millions of Americans, because we all have at least one thing in common: We aspire to something more in our lives for ourselves and our families.

Your 30-Day Millionaire Zone
Getting Started Program

All of the quizzes and worksheets referenced here are available at themillionairezone.com

Days 1–4: The Millionaire Zone Profile (30 minutes plus)
Visit www.themillionairezone.com and complete the Millionaire Zone Profile. This will be your starting point. Just like a compass, it is designed to set you in the right direction, to help you determine the best path for reaching the Millionaire Zone. Once you've received your Millionaire Zone Profile, read it, reflect on it. What does it say about you? Is it accurate? What adjustments might you need to make based on what you know about youself?

Days 5–7: Wire Your LifeNet (3 days, 30 minutes each)
I want you to devote some time to thinking about the people, places, and resources at your disposal. Start by completing the LifeNet diagram on the next page. For each circle in your LifeNet, try to identify at least five people, places, or resources. You did this in Chapter 3 so you can either copy what you listed there or start from scratch here. Don't worry for the moment about how these resources will help you. For now, just list who they are and what you know about them. After you've spent your first 30 minutes on this exercise, take time to think about your list, then come back to it another day. Think about it as you're driving, walking, or doing other activities and watch your mind expand at the possibilities within your LifeNet and the possibilities for reaching the Millionaire Zone.

Days 8–14: Turn Passions into Profits
(2–3 hours over several days)
Remember your list of passions you created in Chapter 6? Pull them out. During this week, I want you to think about those things you wrote down. Our goal will be to turn the things that stir you

Your LifeNet

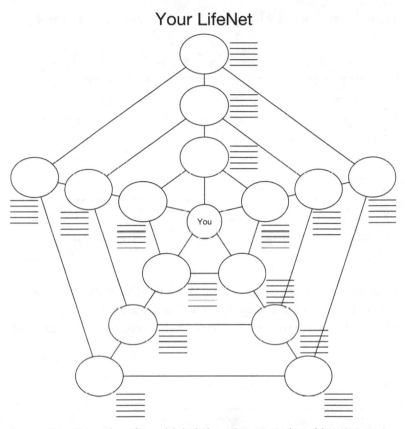

Figure 9.   First, identify and label the primary circles of key categories of people, places, and resources. They may be the same as or different from those in our original LifeNet diagram. Then, identify at least five people, places, or resources within each category that might be helpful in some way.

most deeply into profitable ideas. We will also help you identify any missing ingredients in your otherwise winning recipe for mixing those passions with real world strategies.

STEP 1: LIST YOUR PASSIONS (15 MINUTES)

Take your passion list from Chapter 6 and write it below. Feel free to change or add to your list. After all, the more you list, the more your mind will open up to the many opportunities you have.

1. _____

2. _____

3. _____

4. _____

5. _____

6. _____

7. _____

8. _____

9. _____

10. _____

Looking at the above list, pick three items which you care most about in your life. Put another way, if you had to spend ten years on a desert island, which three passions would you fight hardest to keep with you?
    My top 3 passions are:

1. _____

2. _____

3. _____

Step 2: Turn Passions to Profitable Ideas (30 minutes)

From your top three passions, brainstorm the many ways you can make money with them. Your Millionaire Zone Profile will have given you some ideas of places to start. If you're not sure or you're having trouble, reach out to your LifeNet. Start by turning to the people in your Home Zone to generate money-making ideas. List those ideas in the table on the next page.

Step 3: Identify Power Ideas (15 minutes)

To see if your skills and knowledge can turn any of those ideas into profitable ventures, choose your top three Power Ideas. A Power

Example: Travel	Passion #1	Passion #2	Passion #3
Books on travel to my favorite places			
Cooking school in my favorite city			
Kiosk in airports where people can make last-minute hotel/car plans			
Coupon book to save on restaurants in most traveled areas in Europe			
Web site to sell travel accessories			
Web site to connect people to best-priced travel accessories			
Manufacture travel kit with essential "liquids" (shampoo, sunscreen) for sale near baggage claim/ arrival area			

Idea is one that fills a market need and from which you can make significant money by addressing that need. Take a few lines to describe your Power Ideas and specifically how they will make money. We described one Power Idea for Kristine in Chapter 10—the one about starting Tutor Today USA in her hometown and then branching out across the country.

Power Idea #1	Power Idea #2	Power Idea #3
_____	_____	_____
_____	_____	_____
_____	_____	_____

STEP 4: LIST SKILLS AND KNOWLEDGE (30 MINUTES)
For each Power Idea, list the skills and knowledge you will need. You know from your work in Chapter 6 which skills and knowledge you already have. This will help you identify gaps you will need to fill to be successful.

Example: Travel Lotions Kit

Skills:	*Knowledge:*
Marketing	Vendors to supply materials
Packaging	Travel needs
Promotion	Distributors
Manufacturing	Competitors

Example: Remodeling Homes

Skills:	*Knowledge:*
Painting	Population trends/growth areas
Construction	Construction costs
Interior design	Financing techniques

Power Idea #1 _____

My Skills	*My Knowledge*
_____	_____
_____	_____
_____	_____
_____	_____
_____	_____
_____	_____
_____	_____
_____	_____

Power Idea #2 _____

My Skills

_____

_____

_____

_____

_____

_____

_____

My Knowledge

_____

_____

_____

_____

_____

_____

_____

Power Idea #3 _____

My Skills

_____

_____

_____

_____

_____

_____

_____

My Knowledge

_____

_____

_____

_____

_____

_____

_____

STEP 5: IDENTIFY YOUR GAPS (30 MINUTES)

For each Power Idea, identify your gaps—the skills and knowledge which you do not bring to the table and need to fill in to make your venture work.

Now, refer back to Day 5 and your LifeNet. Look at it. Who and what can help you fill those gaps? Think about not just people and organizations, but the classes, conferences, and seminars you can attend. Filling those gaps is essential to being successful but so is having the best Power Idea.

Power Idea #1:	Power Idea #2:	Power Idea #3:
Gap:	Gap:	Gap:
Filler:	Filler:	Filler:
Gap:	Gap:	Gap:
Filler:	Filler:	Filler:
Gap:	Gap:	Gap:
Filler:	Filler:	Filler:
Gap:	Gap:	Gap:
Filler:	Filler:	Filler:
Gap:	Gap:	Gap:
Filler:	Filler:	Filler:

STEP 6: CHOOSE YOUR MILLIONAIRE ZONE POWER IDEA (15 MINUTES)

For each idea, we want to ask a series of key questions to determine which is the most viable. See the chart on the next page. For each statement to the left, assign a 1–5 score with 5 being a clear "yes," 3 being "unsure," and 1 being "no." For example, if there is a strong market need for the product or service described in Power Idea #1, you would place a 5 in the space under Power Idea #1. You may have to do some additional research to answer these questions or you may already have the knowledge.

The Power Idea with the highest score is the one you should consider taking to the next step. You can always revisit these ideas if you face some unexpected challenges.

Days 15–21: Form LifeNet Partnerships (5 hours plus)

Once you've zoomed in on your #1 Power Idea, during this week, you will be talking to the members of your LifeNet about your Power Idea. Your goal is to:

1. *Gain feedback on your Power Idea*—what do they think of it? What information does this person or organization have that

	Power Idea #1	Power Idea #2	Power Idea #3
Market Need People will want my product or service.			
Customers People will pay for my product or service.			
Pricing Power I will be able to increase prices or sell more of my product or service.			
Competition I can distinguish myself from any competitors.			
Obsolescence My product/ service will not become obsolete or be replaced by technology.			
Barriers to Entry It will be difficult for someone else to duplicate.			
Gaps I can fill the gaps I've identified above (in Step 5).			
Total Add all of the above.			

can help you? What relationships does this person or organization have that can help move you forward?

2. Help fill those gaps listed above—does this person or organization have resources you need? Might they be a likely partner? Remember the lessons learned in Chapter 8 on care and feeding of your LifeNet.

Start this week by listing 10 people with skills or knowledge related to your Power Idea. Plan to meet with each contact for at least 30 minutes to help gain feedback and fill your gaps. Refer to your LifeNet from Week 1 to identify these people and organizations or connect with others at www.themillionairezone.com.

10 Members of My LifeNet to Contact

1. _____
2. _____
3. _____
4. _____
5. _____
6. _____
7. _____
8. _____
9. _____
10. _____

HONING YOUR "ELEVATOR PITCH"

People have short attention spans. It's just a fact of life. So you need to perfect your elevator pitch—those two or three sentences that succinctly tell someone (in the time it takes to ride with them in an elevator) what your idea is, how it will make money and why anyone should care. Make sure the tone of your pitch matches your commitment. You want people to know it's a serious career change, not just some idea that popped into your head five minutes ago.

Example: Travel Cleaning Kit: I've got a great idea for people who want to clean their clothes while they're traveling. It's a travel kit we'll sell in airports for $19.95. It'll have everything in it to dry clean, wash, and iron clothes. There's nothing out there like it.

Write your elevator pitch here: _____

_____

_____

Day 22: Create Demand: The Millionaire Zone Pipeline
(1 hour)

Now that you've chosen your Power Idea, it's time to create demand—to begin to build and fill your pipeline of money. Here, we want to identify ways you can really turn your passions into profits.

LIST 10 CUSTOMERS FOR YOUR PRODUCT/SERVICE

Which customers will you be selling your product to? Will you be going direct or through distributors or other wholesalers? List 10 potential customers for your product or service.

My 10 Potential Customers

1. _____
2. _____
3. _____
4. _____
5. _____
6. _____
7. _____
8. _____
9. _____
10. _____

LIST 10 POTENTIAL CUSTOMERS FROM YOUR LIFENET

Do the same as above but list those people or organizations recommended by those in your LifeNet.

My 10 Potential Customers

1. _____

2. _____

3. _____

4. _____

5. _____

6. _____

7. _____

8. _____

9. _____

10. _____

LIST 10 PLACES TO GET THE WORD OUT

Think of trade shows, conferences, seminars, publications, or organizations in and beyond your LifeNet where you can offer or tell about your product or service.

10 Places to Get the Word Out

1. _____

2. _____

3. _____

4. _____

5. _____

6. _____

7. _____

8. _____

9. _____

10. _____

As you come across new opportunities, add them to your pipeline. Following my advice in Chapter 6, don't forget to make notes of the people and organizations you meet and the information they share. That very small step will expand your LifeNet and put you one step closer to the Millionaire Zone.

Day 23–25: Create a Budget (2–3 hours)
Remember in Chapter 11, and throughout the book, the ways we discussed to get a project going. Now that you know what your Power Idea is and you're confident you can create demand, let's look at what it will take to get it going. Let's create a budget. I want you to list all the costs you will have every month. Take a first stab at the list, then spend a couple of days noodling on it to make sure you've covered everything.

Expense Category	*Monthly Cost*
Development (product/service related such as production, fulfillment)	
Technology (Web site, hosting)	
Sales/Marketing (logo, advertising, newsletter service, PR)	
Equipment (computers)	
Office (rent, phone, utilities)	
Personnel (salaries)	
Other (legal, insurance)	

Day 26: LifeNet Resources (1 hour)
Now, looking at your budget, are there any resources your LifeNet can provide? Go to your zones in your LifeNet chart. Stop and think who might be able to provide some support and try to think of ways they can benefit in return from you or your new venture.

Days 27–29: Set Goals (2–3 hours)
Use the time line below to set goals to get your venture going and move you to the Millionaire Zone. Don't focus on small daily

GOALS

Month 1	
Month 2	
Month 3	
Month 4	
Month 5	
Month 6	
Month 7	
Month 8	
Month 9	
Month 10	
Month 11	
Month 12	

tasks but rather key accomplishments you need to have happen in order to go to the next level. Maybe in the first month you want to do a more complete business plan or get a sample of your product made for initial feedback. To make a sample, you need to find an appropriate vendor and have a drawing or some other sketch of your concept. Starting those tasks might fall under Month 1 with the Month 2 goal being to have your sample completed and form an advisory board. You don't have to fill all the boxes; just put the key goals you want for each month as far out as possible. You should update this plan each month.

Day 30: On Your Mark, Get Set, Go

Great job! Take a deep breath and pat yourself on the back. You are now ready to move forward. However, we're not done yet. To move forward and to be successful, as I've stressed throughout this book, you need to have support around you.

The Millionaire Zone Network

People who are already successful entrepreneurs or executives belong to member-based organizations that provide networking and resource opportunities. These organizations have been critical to providing support, resources, and contacts that help people reach the Millionaire Zone and overcome obstacles along the way. At www.themillionairezone.com, I've created a place where you can meet, connect, and expand your LifeNet. There you can find others who can provide feedback, fill your gaps, serve as partners, or even help introduce you to others. You'll find information, tools, and direct links to programs to help you make money and get support in the process. Join me at www.themillionairezone.com and start making it happen.

· 13 ·

Conclusion

"We're all working together; that's the secret."

—Sam Walton

While this is the conclusion of *The Millionaire Zone* book, it's just the beginning of your incredibly exciting journey to the Millionaire Zone itself. I promise you're going to discover more about yourself and your world than you ever thought possible.

And as you go, keep this book handy. Flip through its pages as you need, to help remind you of all the strategies discussed here. From wiring your LifeNet, to moving your Comfort Zone, to using your Home Zone to find your passions and turning them into profits, to creating demand for your business, to nurturing your LifeNet, to transforming rejection into acceptance—you've got the most powerful tools imaginable to help you along the way.

And when the going gets tough, as it inevitably will at times, go back through the stories you've read, remembering:

Desma Reid-Coleman, who bounced back from a broken marriage to start up three successful ventures, all using ideas from her closest friends;

Mark Fitzgerald, who conquered his fear of leaving his Comfort Zone by partnering with a coworker and, ultimately, building one of the biggest shoe retailers online;

Wayne Finkel, with his wife, Charlene Rios, whose auditing acumen allowed him to assemble his own multimillion-dollar firm, with the company he left becoming his first customer;

Marnie Walker, who founded a transportation business which helped those afflicted with the same kind of disabilities she had suffered as a young woman;

Erica Zohar, who discovered a world of women who, like her, wanted smart-looking, comfortable, stylish casual clothes and ended up running a fast-growing apparel enterprise;

Bob Lorsch, who turned a no into a billion-dollar prepaid calling card operation, and who now never misses an opportunity to say yes to people around him;

Kevin DiCerbo, who epitomized the gritty entrepreneur, persisting through rejection after rejection, to finally finance his extremely successful skin-treatment centers.

As extraordinary as their accomplishments are—and there are thousands of other stories like these out there—these are ordinary people like you and me. The one big difference is that you have an advantage they didn't have. You've read this book. Now you can take the lessons you've learned from these Zoners, as well as the examples of their energy, creativity, and resourcefulness, to achieve your dreams and ambitions. After all, while *The Millionaire Zone* is dedicated to the idea that no one can do it alone, what's behind all the people and successes you've read about in these pages is still just plain old hard work. Their drive is an essential part of the American spirit and character—that is *not* a myth.

I truly hope this book inspires you to follow in their footsteps.